ANALYTIC SYNTAX

D0863209

ANALYTIC SYNTAX

Otto Jespersen

With an Introduction by
James D. McCawley

The University of Chicago Press

The University of Chicago Press, Chicago 60637

© 1984 by the University of Chicago Press
All rights reserved. Published 1937
University of Chicago Press edition 1984
Printed in the United States of America

93 92 91 90 89 88 87 86 85 84   5 4 3 2 1

The Introduction is based, in part, on ideas previously published in the review of *Analytic Syntax*, by Otto Jespersen, in *Language* 46 (1970): 442–449.

CONTENTS

PART II   COMMENTS

INTRODUCTION

James D. McCawley

As Jespersen's *Analytic Syntax* again comes back into print, I can for a second time cross it off the top of my list of important out-of-print linguistics books. I hope that it will not become eligible to hold that position of honor a third time; better that it should have a different honor that it deserves more but so far has been denied: that of remaining continuously in print and being widely read.

I first heard of *Analytic Syntax* (henceforth, *AS*) in Edward S. Klima's "Structure of English" course at M.I.T. in autumn 1961, where it was recommended to the students as an unparalleled source of insight into English syntax, but it was not until five or six years later that I actually followed Klima's advice and read *AS*. Since *AS* consists mainly of example sentences and formulaic analyses, it is not a book that one might expect to read from cover to cover in just a couple of sittings, but I did exactly that, with fascination that increased as I progressed from each group of formulas to the next. Jespersen, 20 years before the beginnings of transformational grammar (*AS* was originally published in 1937), had dealt with many of the same syntactic phenomena that were occupying transformational grammarians, had given analyses that had much in common with what in the mid-60s were the latest and hottest ideas in transformational grammar, and had gone in considerable depth into many important syntactic phenomena that merited but had not yet received the attention of transformational grammarians.

AS represents *He promised her to go* and *He allowed her to go* as differing with regard to whether the 'latent' subject of *go* is coreferential with *he* or with *her* (p. 49), and *the advance of science* and *the advancement of science* as differing with regard to whether *science* is the subject or object of the nominalization (p. 58):

(1) a. He promised her to go. S V O O(S°I)
   a'. He allowed her to go. S V O O(S$_2^\circ$(O)I)
   b. The advance of science. X pS
   b'. The advancement of science. X pO

(In these formulas, the $^\circ$ indicates 'latent,' i.e. 'understood,' and repeated relation letters are used to specify coreferentiality, so that the repeated S in (la) indicates an understood NP coreferential to the subject and the repeated *O* in (1b) an understood NP coreferential to the indirect object.) *AS* gives an analysis of *John is easy to deceive* in which *John* is represented as both surface subject of *is* and underlying object of *deceive* (p. 52), an analysis of *She seems to notice it* in which *she to notice it* is a sentential subject of *seem* (p. 47), and an analysis of *I am not sure he is ill* in which the complement is the object of an understood preposition (p. 62):

(2) a. John is easy to deceive. S(O*) V P(2 pI*)
    b. She seems to notice it. $\frac{1}{2}$S V $\frac{1}{2}$S(IO)
    c. I am not sure he is ill. S V^n P p^o1(S_2 V P_2)

Some important things that *AS* helped me to see for the first time are the possibility of prepositional phrases serving as subject or object (p. 22), the existence of understood prepositions and conjunctions in several kinds of compound words (pp. 17–19), and the sentential nature of certain seemingly nonsentential NP's (p. 42):

(3) a. You have till ten tonight. S V O(p13)
    b. Franco-Prussian war 2(2&^{o}-2) 1
    c. Too many cooks spoil the broth. S($3PS_2$) V O

In (3c), for example, *cooks* is treated as the subject of *too many*, as it would be in the semi-sentence **Cooks being too many spoils the broth*.[1]

    In the intervening years, I have come to realize that Jespersen's scheme of syntactic analysis was not as close to that of mid-60s transformational grammar as I had thought. The current approach to syntax with which *AS* has the most in common is in fact RELATIONAL GRAMMAR (Perlmutter 1983, Perlmutter and Rosen 1984), in which grammatical relations such as 'subject' and 'direct object' are taken as conceptual primitives, and a syntactic analysis is regarded not (as in orthodox transformational grammar) as a sequence of syntactic structures (a deep structure, a surface structure, and various intermediate structures) but as a single structure in which underlying and surface grammatical relations are represented together. For example, the formula in (2a) conveys much the same information as does the relational diagram (4):

---

[1] The sentential status of *too many cooks* in (3c) is particularly clear for those idiolects in which singular number agreement is preferred: *Too many cooks spoils the broth;* cf. Ross's argument (1969b:256) that *which problems* is a reduced form of the clause *which problems he's going to give us* in the sentence, *He's going to give us some old problems for the test, but which problems isn't/*aren't clear.*

(4)

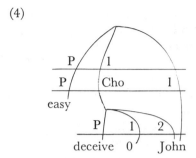

Both (2a) and (4) represent *John* as underlying object of *deceive* (Jespersen's O means the same thing as the 2 of relational grammar), and both represent it as the surface subject of the main clause, though they differ regarding exactly what is predicated of it in surface structure (note that *easy to deceive* is represented as a 'predicate' in (2a) but not in (4)).[2]

In any event, though, many of Jespersen's analyses embody ideas that lend themselves to exploitation in transformational grammar, as in (2a), where the idea of the surface subject of *be* being the underlying object of the infinitive can be recast in the form of the transformation of Tough-movement, which extracts a NP from an embedded nonfinite VP and (in one formulation) puts it in place of an expletive *it*.[3] Likewise, his treatment of *seem, fail, happen,* and *be sure* as having a discontinuous sentential subject can be recast in the form of a Raising transformation, in which the subject of a complement clause is made into a derived subject of the main clause.

I will devote the bulk of this foreword to details of Jespersen's notational practices that require some clarification, in the hope of rendering his ideas more accessible to the reader. Jespersen's formulas, while embodying much information that in standard transformational analyses would be matters of deep structure, are best described as 'annotated surface structures.' Each formula consists of a string of

[2] Also, (4) but not (2a) indicates explicitly that *to deceive* is a surface 'chômeur': a constituent that has lost an underlying grammatical relation as a concomitant of another constituent taking over that relation, here as a concomitant of *John* taking over the subject relation.

[3] One respect in which this treatment of *easy to deceive* does not exactly match Jespersen's is that Jespersen gives *It is easy to deceive John* an analysis (s V P S(IO)) in which the infinitive is outside the 'predicate' constituent, whereas in his (2a) the infinitive and the adjective jointly comprise a 'predicate.' The Tough-movement transformation does not provide for such a difference.

symbols and brackets and indicates (subject to some qualifications) surface immediate constituent structure, 'latent' (= 'understood') elements, coreferentiality relations, and both superficial and underlying grammatical relations.

Constituent structure is indicated only partially, with parentheses and the presence or absence of spaces specifying those details of constituent structure that Jespersen found it convenient to indicate, but with no attempt made to represent the structure in full. A great many details of constituent structure have been left out of the formulas, though much of the evidence for this assertion must come from a comparison with other works from Jespersen's later years. For example, his formula for *John and Mary came*, S_1 & S_2 V (p. 112), contains no indication that *John and Mary* is even a constituent, let alone the subject of *come*. However, since *AS* is full of comments about points on which Jespersen has changed his mind, and he had stated emphatically only a few years earlier that the conjuncts of a conjoined subject are not each individually subjects,[4] we can conclude from the absence of any indication that the formula represents a change of mind that he takes *John and Mary* to be the subject of *come*, which he could have represented (but for unknown reasons didn't) with the formula S(1 & 1) V, or perhaps (if he wished to adopt an analog to a Conjunction-reduction analysis) $S(S_1$ & $S_2)$ V. Likewise, while (2b) does not indicate the status of *seems to notice it* as a surface constituent, or of *she* as a surface subject, Jespersen must intend *she* to be taken as a surface subject, in view of statements to that effect on page 47 and in 1933:107–8.

One point on which Jespersen's incomplete representation of constituent structure is liable to misinterpretation is that of how auxiliary verbs fit into surface constituent structure. Jespersen usually ignores an auxiliary verb when it is adjacent to the verb with which it is connected and represents it with a *v* when it is separated from the main verb. However, he states (p. 92) that he regards auxiliary verbs as true verbs, having their own subjects and objects, and occasionally writes formulas as in (5) in which that syntactic role for the auxiliary verb is made explicit:

(5) a. He will drink whisky. S V O(I O_2)
   b. He has been drinking whisky. S V O(Y P(Y_2 O_2))
   c. He was loved. S V P(Y^b)

---

[4] 'In *The cat and the dog do not agree very well*, there are not two grammatical subjects, but *the cat and the dog* together is the subject, as will be seen from a comparison with the synonymous [*sic*] expression *They do not agree very well*' (1933:97).

He describes (5a-b) as 'a more explicit but inconvenient way of symbolising' what he usually writes as simply S V O and speaks of his practice of writing S V^b instead of (5c) as 'a practical but harmless simplification, similar in character to that which makes us write *has killed, will kill*, etc. simply as V.' Jespersen's analysis of auxiliary verbs is thus very close to that of Ross 1969*c*, in which auxiliary verbs have the syntactic as well as the morphological characteristics of verbs, but his abbreviated notations give many of his formulas the appearance of an analysis like that of Chomsky 1957, in which auxiliary verbs are treated as *sui generis*.

Jespersen represents 'understood' elements in the positions where items with the same syntactic function would appear if expressed overtly, with any grammatical relations or coreferentiality relations in which they participate indicated explicitly, e.g.:

(6) He is dressing. S V O°(S)

The parenthesized S indicates that the 'latent' direct object is coreferential with the subject. (If Jespersen had meant that that element itself stood in a subject relation, he would have written S_2* rather than S, with paired asterisks indicating what it was subject of.) Another notational device of Jespersen's overlaps somewhat in applicability with the °, namely his braces to indicate that a single word incorporates elements with separate syntactic roles. It is not clear to me why Jespersen invokes the one device in (7a) and the other in (7b), both taken from his page 7:

(7) a. (Italian) Canta. 'He sings' S° V
   b. (Latin) Amo puellam. 'I love the girl' {SV} O

With the brace notation, Jespersen adheres to his policy of writing elements in the order in which they would appear if they were expressed by separate words, even when that conflicts with the order of the morphemes within the word represented:

(8) a. (Finnish) purteni 'my boat' {1²1}
   b. (Portuguese) É triste combateres. 'It is a pity that you fight'
      V P S({S_2I})

The *-ni* of (8a) corresponds to the 1² (primary converted into secondary, e.g., genitive) and the *-es* of (8b) corresponds to the subject of the infinitive.[5]

---

[5] The occasional instances where Jespersen writes 'latent' elements in positions

The repeated relation symbol S in (6) is one of two ways in which Jespersen indicated coreferentiality. Specifically, he repeated S, O, or *O* to indicate that a pronoun or a 'latent' element had the subject, direct object, or indirect object as its antecedent. Otherwise he used his ubiquitous asterisks to mark coreferentiality,[6] as in:

(9) a. (French) Il me le donne a moi. 'He gives it to me' S *O** O V [pl*] (p. 37)

    b. Zionism—what is that to me? [1*] P? V S* pl. (p. 35)

    c. Come here at once, Mary! $\{$S*V$\}$ 3 3 [1*]! (p. 38)

For example, the asterisks in (9c) indicate that the vocative is coreferential with the understood subject of the imperative (treated here as fused with the verb). His formulas for six readings of *John told Robert's son that he must help him* (p. 26) make liberal use of both asterisks and repeated relation symbols in representing the various coreferentiality relations.

Jespersen's notions of nexus, junction, and rank, which I have alluded to above several times, merit some discussion. Nexus and junction are two ways in which elements of a sentence can be combined, differing in that the parts of a nexus are connected by 'grammatical relations' such as 'subject of,' while the parts of a junction are connected only by 'dependency relations' such as 'modifies.' While a nexus can often be treated as an underlying sentence, Jespersen does not appear to have intended that all nexi be so treated. He thus anticipated Chomsky's treatment (Chomsky 1970 and subsequent works) of nominalizations as involving parallel relations among the parts of a NP to those among the parts of a sentence, e.g.,[7]

---

other than where overt counterparts would occur may be slips on his part, e.g.: To see is to believe. S(IS°∞) V P(IS°∞). (The ∞ of this formula, apparently meaning 'generic,' was inadvertently omitted from the list of symbols that comprises chapter 2 of *AS*.)

[6] Besides indicating what a given element is connected to by a grammatical relation, as in (2a), and indicating coreferentiality, as in (9), asterisks occasionally indicate scopes of quantifiers and negations: All men are not born to reign. S(2q*1) V 3n* P(YpI) (p. 26).

[7] The O in (10) expresses a relation to the 'nexus substantive' (X) *massacres*, not to the preposition *of*. Where most linguists speak of the 'object' of a preposition, Jespersen speaks of its 'regimen'; he writes 'pO' only in cases where the 'regimen' of the preposition stands in the object relation to a verb or a nominalization. Jespersen indicates grammatical relations to a nexus substantive even when the constituent in question is separated from the remainder of the nominalization, e.g.: J'en vois la necessite. 'I see the necessity of it' S 2(S₂)* V O(X*) (p. 58). (The 2 in this formula may be a typographical error for 3; elsewhere, e.g., p. 31, Jespersen

(10) massacres of Christians by Chinese X pO pS (p. 58)

The notion of dependency on which Jespersen based his idea of 'junction' is one of dependency between constituents of arbitrary complexity, not the standard notion of traditional grammar, in which a dependency relation can hold only, or at least, typically, between two words.[8] Chains of dependency relations determine 'ranks,' with 'primaries,' i.e., items of rank 1, at the bottom of all chains of dependencies. Elements of rank 2 ('secondaries') are dependent on elements of rank 1, elements of rank 3 ('tertiaries') are dependent on elements of rank 2, etc. Since Jespersen took verbs to be dependent on their subjects and objects, those subjects and objects are primaries and verbs are secondaries.[9] He in fact takes NP's to be primaries even when they are not serving as subjects or objects. In addition, he takes nouns to be primaries, so that in (11) we have three primaries: *she* (converted into a secondary by the genitive inflection), *eyes*, and the whole NP *her eyes*, on which *are* is dependent:

(11) Her eyes are blue. S($1^2$1) V P

Jespersen remarks (p. 123) that according to his system of ranks, corresponding parts of (12a) and (12b) have the same ranks.

(12) a. The dog barked furiously.
    b. the furiously barking dog
    c. the furious barking of the dog

He does not comment, however, on the fact that in (12c) *barking* and *furious* differ in rank from their counterparts in (12a-b), e.g., *barking* in (12c) is a primary. I see no plausible way in which a consistent notion of rank could make all three of these constructions parallel as regards rank.

Rank is indeed the one major notion in *AS* that I doubt can be worked out in a way that is both internally consistent and consistent with Jespersen's claims. It is particularly difficult to apply the notion

---

treats *en* as a tertiary. I have added a subscript 2 on the second S, as Jespersen's notational scheme demands.)

[8] On the history of notions of dependency and constituent structure, see Percival 1976. Percival argues that Bloomfield, who did the most to popularize immediate constituent structure as the central notion of syntactic structure, got the idea from Wilhelm Wundt.

[9] Aside from a verb being simultaneously dependent on its subject and objects, Jespersen allows an element to be dependent on at most one thing at a time.

of rank to predicate adjectives. Jespersen speaks of them as being secondaries but also seems to regard them as standing in some dependency relation with the copula, which would make them either primaries or tertiaries (depending on which direction the relation goes), since the copula is for Jespersen a secondary. The only at all obvious way out of that difficult would be to adopt an analysis that Jespersen explicitly rejects (pp. 132–5): Hammerich's proposal (or the essentially equivalent analysis in Ross 1969a) that the copula is an intransitive verb having a sentential subject of the form NP + Adj (e.g., in *The horse is sick*, the [underlying] subject of *is* is *The horse sick*).

But I should not overemphasize one of the few ideas in *AS* that appears not to be viable. As I approach the end of this introduction, I should return to the delight that I have derived from reading *AS* and express my hope that by alerting readers to what lies behind its initially intimidating notational system I may have helped them to share in that delight.

AS is one of Jespersen's last works: it was completed when he was 77 years old, and most of the remaining six years of his life were devoted to work on the fifth, sixth, and unfinished seventh volumes of his *Modern English Grammar on Historical Principles. AS* gives the most concentrated dose of syntactic analysis to be found in the whole Jespersen canon and presents an integrated summary of the syntactic research that had engaged much of his efforts for 50 years.[10] Its position among his works can perhaps best be likened to the position among Bach's works of the B minor mass, a work that Bach put together late in his life out of arrangements of movements from many of his cantatas. In both cases the result is a monumental work in which a major creative figure surveys his output in a genre that was particularly close to his heart. I hope that the appearance of this reprint as *AS* will speed the arrival of the day when ignorance of *Analytic Syntax* on the part of a linguist will be as unthinkable as ignorance of the B minor mass on the part of a musical scholar.

---

[10] The breadth and profundity of Jespersen's syntactic research, however, should not be allowed to eclipse his major contributions to virtually all other fields of linguistics, most notably phonetics, language change, language acquisition, and language planning.

REFERENCES

Chomsky, Noam A. 1957. *Syntactic Structures*. The Hague: Mouton.
———. 1970. "Remarks on Nominalization." In R. Jacobs and P. S.

Rosenbaum, eds., *Readings in English Transformational Grammar* (Washington: Georgetown University Press), 184–221.

Jespersen, Otto. 1933. *Essentials of English Grammar*. London: Allen and Unwin.

Percival, W. Keith. 1976. "On the Historical Source of Immediate Constituent Analysis." In J. McCawley, ed., *Notes from the Linguistic Underground* (Syntax and Semantics 7) (New York: Academic Press), 229–42.

Perlmutter, David M. 1983. *Studies in Relational Grammar* 1. Chicago: University of Chicago Press.

Perlmutter, David M., and Carol Rosen. 1984. *Studies in Relational Grammar* 2. Chicago: University of Chicago Press.

Ross, John Robert. 1969a. "Adjectives as Noun Phrases." *Modern Studies in English*, edited by D. Reibel and S. Schane, 352–60. Englewood Cliffs, N.J.: Prentice-Hall.

———. 1969b. "Guess Who?" *Papers from the Fifth Regional Meeting of the Chicago Linguistic Society*, edited by R. Binnick et al., 252–86. Chicago: Linguistics Dept., University of Chicago.

———. 1969c. "Auxiliaries as Main Verbs." *Studies in Philosophical Linguistics*, ser. 1, edited by Wm. Todd, 77–102. Evanston, Ill.: Great Expectations.

PREFACE

This book may be considered the crowning effort of many years' occupation with grammatical problems and thus forms a kind of supplement to my "Philosophy of Grammar" (abbreviated PhilGr) and "The System of Grammar." I sincerely hope that fellow-students will not let themselves be deterred by the look of my seemingly abstruse formulas, but will study them closely enough to realize their value in making it possible to gain a deeper insight into grammatical constructions in general. My system forces one to consider many things and enables one to express them succinctly; let me mention only two examples: the difference between *usually* and *unusually* in 10.2, and that between the infinitives after *promise* and *allow* 17.2. It should also prove useful in comparing the grammatical structure of languages not considered in this volume.

I want to thank some friends who have assisted me in various ways. Dr. F. Ohrt has aided me with what I say about Finnish—a language which I studied with Vilh. Thomsen more than thirty years ago, but have since then nearly completely forgotten. Mr. F. Y. Thompson, M.A., has kindly read parts of my book and has suggested some improvements in my English style. The greatest debt of gratitude, however, I owe to some young Danish linguists, to whom I have shown my system, or parts of it, at various stages of its completion, Poul Christophersen, Niels Haislund, Louis L. Hammerich, Aage Hansen. Not only has their kind criticism saved me from some pitfalls into which I might otherwise have fallen, but on some points they have even suggested things which I have been glad to embody in my system. To Niels Haislund I owe special thanks for the care with which throughout the whole of my work he has transcribed my notes, checked my analyses and finally read the proofs—not always an easy task. Finally, I am greatly obliged to the Directors of the Carlsberg Foundation for their support of my scientific work.

And now, with apology for some inconsistencies which I have not been able to avoid, I may say with one of my quotations:

Libro completo, saltat auctor pede laeto.

Lundehave, Helsingør.   Otto Jespersen
1937

PART I

SYMBOLS AND EXAMPLES

Language-makers, that is ordinary speakers, are not very accurate thinkers. But neither are they devoid of a certain natural logic.

Phil. of Gr. 81.

CHAPTER 1.

Introduction.

An attempt is made in the present volume at devising a system of succinct and in part self-interpreting syntactic formulas. By means of letters, chiefly initials of ordinary grammatical terms, numerals, and a few more or less arbitrary signs it has been made possible to denote all the most important *interrelations of words and parts of words in connected speech,* even some which are hardly touched upon in ordinary grammars.

It will be seen that what is aimed at is to some extent similar to the well-known symbols used in chemistry, C standing for Carbon and H_2O for water (two atoms of hydrogen to one of oxygen), etc. In phonetics my own Antalphabetic (formerly called Analphabetic) system[1] provides analogous means for symbolizing the formation of speech-sounds, in which Greek letters stand for the active organs of speech (lips, tip of the tongue, etc.), numerals for the degree and form of the opening, if any (0 = closure, 1, 2, 3, etc. for gradually more open sounds), small Latin letters for the place of articulation, so that, for instance, the vowel in E. *full* is analyzed as $\alpha 3^b$ $\beta,, \gamma 4^j \delta 0$ $\varepsilon 1$.

The symbols here introduced also to some extent resemble the wonderful system of symbols which during the last few centuries has contributed so much to make mathematics (and in some degree logic) exact and more easy to manage than was possible with the unwieldy word-descriptions used formerly. My system aims at providing linguists with some of the same advantages; but it cannot pretend to the same degree of universality as either the chemical or mathematical symbols. This is precluded simply because of the fact, which it is no use shirking, that *language is everywhere socially*

---

[1] See *Lehrbuch der Phonetik* (B. G. Teubner, Leipzig) and *Essentials of Phonetics* (to be published by G. Allen & Unwin, London).

conditioned: even those things which to a superficial observer would seem to be absolutely indispensable in any language used to express human thought are not found everywhere in the same way. The more the so-called primitive or "exotic" languages are studied, the more we have come to realize that much of what we are accustomed from our schooldays and from the best-known languages to consider inherent in all human language is totally foreign to other types of language, which nevertheless are wonderful instruments to express the ideas and feelings of the peoples brought up in them. My system was at first devised with special regard to the grammatical structure of English and still preserves traces of this, more particularly through the disproportionate number of English examples, though I have afterwards tried to apply it to some other languages. Now it is my hope that others will find it useful, possibly with some alterations and extensions, even to analyze languages with whose structure I am not at all familiar.

The book is divided into two parts. In Part I (Chapters **1—27**) is given, besides an enumeration of the symbols employed, a series of examples without much comment (except towards the end) according to a principle which I quote at second hand:

> Nur das beispiel führt zum licht;
> Vieles reden tut es nicht.

Part II (Chapters **28** ff.) contains Comments, discussing at some length the chief debatable points and forming in some respects a supplement to and correction of the author's "Philosophy of Grammar".

Something must be said here of the character of the examples given in the following chapters. Some are taken from my reading, some from standard grammars, but not a few are made-up sentences, which I have endeavoured to make idiomatic and terse without much regard to variety in real contents. In spite of all the pains bestowed upon them it may be feared that they have not avoided a certain monotony and even now and then approach that kind of sentences which I have often ridiculed when found in books for teaching foreign languages. My excuse is that this book is not written with a pedagogical purpose in view, but presupposes a previous knowledge of the language from which the example is taken, as well as a theoretical interest in grammar as such. The important thing, therefore, was to find short unambiguous sentences suitable to illustrate the employment and utility of formulas in a multiplicity of grammatical constructions.

Let me add that the elaboration of the present system has opened my eyes to the real character of many things even in the languages I was most familiar with : the complexity of human language and thought is clearly brought before one when one tries to get behind the more or less accidental linguistic forms in order to penetrate to their notional kernel. Much that we are apt to take for granted in everyday speech and consider as simple or unavoidable discloses itself on being translated into symbols as a rather involved logical process, a fact that is shown, for instance, by the number of parentheses necessary in some of the examples.

Many of the sentences I wanted to analyze have been far from easy, and I do not claim to have always found the best solution of the difficulties. Still I thought it better to give my own attempts for what they are worth than to shirk the task. As a matter of fact I have pretty often hesitated and changed the transcription of the same sentences over and over again, and consequently cannot expect that my readers will always agree with my final decision.[1]

It has also been rather a difficult task to find the best order in which to present the material of this book.[2] In some cases it has been found inevitable in early chapters to use symbols the purport of which, though mentioned in Ch. 2, cannot be fully appreciated till a subsequent chapter; but on the whole it is hoped that this will cause no serious inconvenience to the readers, who after all cannot be treated as mere tiros.

The idea is to follow the sentence or word-combination that is to be analyzed word for word. Such combinations, however, as *the man, a man, has taken, will take, is taking*, etc. (generally also *to take*), even *can take*, are reckoned as one unit. Cf. p. 92.

---

[1] Sometimes the analysis has not been carried out to the bitter end, as when *my mind* has been written 1 for simplicity's sake instead of $1(1^21)$. Thus also with some passives, when e.g. F. *était fermé* is written V^b or $V P(Y^b)$ without distinction.

[2] It might, for instance, have been better to collect in one place everything concerning Apposition instead of distributing it among several chapters.

CHAPTER 2.

Symbols.

2. 1. Capitals.

S Subject.

V Verb (finite).

O Object (direct).

O Object (indirect).

E.g. He gave her a ring S V *O* O.

P Predicative: he is angry S V P.

W Composite verbal expression: She waits on us S W O.

I Infinitive.

G Gerund.

X Nexus-substantive, e.g. work, kindness.

Y Agent-substantive or participle, e.g. admirer, admiring, admired.

R Recipient: F. Cela m'est désagréable S R V P.

Z Whole sentence.

If there are in the same sentence two or more subjects, etc., the second (third) may be numbered by a small ₂ (₃) below.
E.g. I consider this a lie S V O(S_2P).

S_x (read cross, not the letter) Reciprocity.
E.g. They hate one another S V O(S_x).

2. 2. Small Letters.

p Preposition.

pp Composite preposition, e.g. on account of.

s "Lesser" subject: It is a pleasure to see you s V P S(IO).

o "Lesser" object.

o "Lesser" indirect object.

v "Lesser" verb (separated from the main verb): Will he come
  v S V.

The reason for these symbols is given in Ch. **28**.4.

The following small letters are placed above as indices:
[a] Active, e.g. S[a] what is subject in an active sentence.
[b] Passive.

^{c} Connective (serving to connect a clause with the principal part of
the sentence, conjunction, relative pronoun, etc.).
^{cc} Composite connective, e.g. in order that.
^{m} Modified (adjunct), see **3**.6.
^{n} Negative.
^{q} Quantifier.
^{r} Result: He digs a hole S V O^r.

2. 3. Numerals Indicate Rank.

1 Primary.
2 Secondary.
3 Tertiary.
4 Quaternary, etc.
E.g. Terribly bad weather 321 (read three two one).
2(3) Secondary that is virtually a tertiary to an adjective or verb
contained in a word: an utter fool 2(3)1.

A raised ^{2} changes a primary into a secondary, e.g. John's
books 1^{2}1.
^{0} (raised cipher) Latent, not expressed, e.g. It. canta 'he sings' S^0 V.
On the small numerals below see **2**.1.
$\frac{1}{2}$ S, $\frac{1}{2}$ O Half-subject, half-object, see Ch. **16**.

2. 4. Brackets.

( ) Particulars serving to explain the item immediately preceding.
E.g. He amuses himself S V O(S)—indicating identity of subject
and object.
{ } Two or more items expressed in the same form.
E.g. L. Amo puellam { SV } O.
[ ] Extraposition or apposition.
E.g. G. Die sterne, die begehrt man nicht [1] O V S 3^n.
Browning, the poet 1 [1].
< > Speaker's aside.
E.g. He fairly screamed S <3> V.

2. 5. Kinds of Sentences.

? Question.
E.g. Who says that? S? V O.

Is that true? V S P ?

❗ Request.
E.g. Come now! $\left\{\begin{array}{c} SV \end{array}\right\}$ 3 ❗.
Out with you! 3 pS❗

!! Wish.
E.g. God bless the King! S V O !!

! Exclamation.
E.g. How dreadful! 3! P S⁰.

2. 6. Auxiliary Signs.

* * Words standing apart, but belonging together.
E.g. L. Maximas tibi gratias ago 2* O O*$\left\{\begin{array}{c} SV \end{array}\right.$.
- Compound of the ordinary type.
E.g. Finger-ring 2-1.
+ Compound of adjective and substantive.
E.g. Holiday 2+1.
+ after a junction: Something added.
E.g. A blue-eyed girl 2(21+)1.
/ Alternative analyses.
E.g. A drunken soldier 2($Y^{b/a}$)1.
There are troubles there 3/s V S 3.
& Coordinating particle.
E.g. Tom and his wife quarrelled S & $S_2(S^21)$ V.
§ Referring to a whole idea (sentence, etc.).
E.g. He gambles, and what is worse, he drinks S V & [$S^c_?VP§$] S V.

2. 7. Languages.

The names of languages from which examples are taken are ab-breviated in this manner (English not marked):
Dan. Danish.
Du. Dutch.
Fi. Finnish.
G. German.
Gk. Greek.

It. Italian.
L. Latin.
Pg. Portuguese.
Ru. Russian (rough transliteration, not phonetic transcription).
Sp. Spanish.
Sw. Swedish.
MEG = the writer's Modern English Grammar.

CHAPTER 3.

Junction.

3. 1. Ordinary Adjuncts.

Old men 21.
The Crown Inn; the Amazon River 21.
Terribly cold weather 321.
Good enough arguments 231.
A not particularly well constructed plot 5^n4321.
So great a man 321; such great men 221.
Astronomer Royal; F. Drapeau rouge; Ru. Dom novyj 'a new house'
$\qquad$ 12.
F. Un temps terriblement froid 132.
F. Un peuple ami, une nation amie 12 (or 11, cf. **3**.5).
My father and brother $1^21\&1^{2o}1$.
My friend and adviser (one person) $1^21(1\&1)$.
A thoroughly German young German $2(32)1(21)$.
Poor old man; perpetual civil war $21(21)$.
Curious little living creatures $21(21(21))$; this symbolization shows
$\qquad$ that *living creatures* is a primary in relation to both the preced-
$\qquad$ ing adjectives, *little living creatures* in the same way with regard
$\qquad$ to *curious*; but no great harm is done by simply writing 2221.
A good-for-nothing fellow $2(2p1)1$.

3. 2. Secondary or Tertiary (cf. MEG II 15.15 and 12.47).

Burning hot soup; wide open windows 2/321.
F. Les fenêtres grandes ouvertes 12/32.
In perfect good temper, in extreme old age $p1(2/321)$.
In high good humour (in the same way, or) $p1(21(21))$.

3. 3. Genitival Adjuncts.

John's hat, my hat 1^21.
   (As already said, the addition of ^{2} turns the 1 into 2.)
John's old hat, my old hat $1^21(21)$, or simply 1^221.
Old John's new hat $1(21)^221$.
Somebody else's hat $1(12)^21$.
His poor mother's heart $1(1^221)^21$, cf. below **6**.3.
His and my uncle $2(1^2 \& 1^2)1$.
For both our sakes $p1(1(21)^21)$.
   Here we may place constructions like
L. Vir summae virtutis $12(21^2)$.
L. Fossa trium pedum $12(2^q1^2)$.
G. Ein gasthof ersten ranges $12(21^2)$.

3. 4. Prepositional Phrases or Adverbs.

The faces of the girls; the peace of God; the father of both; a man
   of honour; a woman of parts; the King of England; the Archbishop of York; a Member of Parliament; secretary to the premier; the man in the moon; women with child $12(p1)$.
F. Le chapeau de Jean; un homme de bien; le roi d'Angleterre;
   (vg.) la vache à papa; du café au lait; un remède pour la
   fièvre $12(p1)$.
Dan. Kongen av Danmark; arving til tronen; manden ved rattet;
   middel mod feber; taget på huset $12(p1)$.
G. Der könig von England; ein man von geschmack; das elend
   von millionen; ein weib aus dem volk; ein konto bei der bank;
   ein vetter von mir; das ding an sich $12(p1)$.
The King of England's castles; Dan. Kongen av Englands slotte
$$1(12(p1))^21.$$

The kind old Archbishop of York's daughter $1(2212(p1))^21$.
It is none of our faults S V $P(1(1p1)^21)$.
Sw. Kungliga Akademiens för de fria konsterna utställningar
$$2(21^*2^*(p21))1.$$

Pre-war prices $2(p1)1$.
An out-of-work joiner $2(ppl)1$.
An old man with one foot in the grave $212(p2^q1p1)$.
Sp. Aquella sin igual mujer 'that peerless woman' $22(p1)1$.

The adjunct may be an adverb:

The then government; the above remark 21.

The man here; Dan. Manden her; G. Der mann dort 12.

A way out 12; cf. G. Ausweg, Dan. Udvej 2-1 (A way out of the difficulty 12(pp1).

3. 5. Equipollent.

In some junctions the two connected items have not, as in the cases so far treated, different rank, but are equipollent. This is especially frequent when a proper name consists of two parts, or when a descriptive (common) name is placed before a proper name:

Baden-Powell; Mary-Ann 11.

Dr. Johnson; Samuel Johnson; King Edward 11.

Captain John Smith 111.

The river Thames 11.

With the opposite word-order we have rather compounds, and the rank is not always easy to determine, see, e.g.,

The Johnson girls; the Brontë sisters 2-1 or 1-1.

See also under Apposition, Ch. **4**, and Compounds, Ch.**6**.

3. 6. Irregular Junction.

(Cf. MEG II Ch. XII).

An adjunct may be virtually a subjunct (tertiary) to some adjectival or verbal idea contained in the primary; this is particularly frequent with X and Y (see Chapters **18** and **19**). We may indicate this by 2(3):

An utter fool; a positive fool; a perfect stranger; an awful swell 2(3)1.

Blackberries were a comparative rarity S V P(2(3)1).

A few absolute necessaries $2^q 2(3)1$.

We were tremendous friends; G. Er war ein starker trinker

S V P(2(3)1).

We were great friends; F. Nous étions de grands amis—may be symbolized in the same way, though there is no corresponding adverb.

G. Ein langjähriger mitarbeiter; Dan. En mangeårig medarbejder 2(3)1, or as in the next paragraph.

3. 7. Implied Predicatives.

In other cases there is an implied predicative-relation in the primary; this may be indicated by a parenthetic P with a star showing the connexion with the adjective:

He is a born poet S V P(2*1(P*)); cf. born as a poet.

G. Eine geborene Rantzau 2*1(P*).

A dismissed director; a deposed king; the former (late) director;
    G. Ein abgesetzter (ehemaliger) direktor; ein gewesener rich-
    ter; Dan. En forhenværende professor 2*1(P*); cf. one who
    has been ...

A future (nominated, designed) bishop; an expectant father; a
    prospective bride 2*1(P*).

F. Le malade imaginaire 1(P*)2* $=$ qui se croit malade.

A seeming widow and a secret bride 2*(Y)1(P*)& 2*1(P*).

3. 8. Unclassifiable.

Some junctions cannot be easily classed; as a symbol we may use ^{m} added to 2 $=$ 'modified'.

A general paralytic 2^{m}1; formed from the regular *general paralysis*.

F. Un paralytique général 12^m.

Cooperative prices 2^{m}1; transferred from *cooperative society*.

A civil servant 2^{m}Y; cf. civil service.

The grand jurors 2^{m}1; cf. grand jury.

In all your born days p1(21^{2}2^{m}1).

In the small hours p1(2^{m}1).

G. In gesunden tagen p1(2^{m}1).

G. Der zoologische bahnhof 2^{m}1(2-1) $=$ der bahnhof am zoolo-
    gischen garten in Berlin.

Dan. Et barn i voxne klær 1p1(2^{m}1).

F. Café chantant; une place assise 12^m.

Her married life 1^2 2^{m}1; better as a compound 1^{2}1(2-1).

An interesting combination is found in cases like "in my young days": *young* does not really qualify *days*, but the "I" inherent in *my*. Therefore we may symbolize (12)^{2}1, if we do not prefer 1^{2}2^{m}1.

3. 9. Secondaries that have become Primaries.

This is shown either by means of the numeral 1 or one of the letters S, O, etc., which imply primary rank.

This hat is mine S(21) V P(1), where 1 = $1^2 1^0$.
The idle rich 21.
The idle rich enjoy life S(21) V O.
The very poor don't enjoy life S(2(3)1) V^n O.
I bought it at the butcher's S V O pl. (Here 1 = $1^2 1^0$).
G. (Pferde). Die weissen sind schöner als die grauen; Dan. De
  hvide er smukkere end de grå S V P 3^c S_2. (Here S = 21^0;
  cf. the white ones 21).
G. Ein schwarzes pferd und vier weisse $2^q 21$ & $2^q 1$.
(Poems). Shelley's are better than Keats's S V P 3^c S_2.
  (Here S and S_2 = $1^2 1^0$).
The out-of-works receive the dole S(pp1) V O.
You are all mine and my all S V P(31) & $P_2(1^2 1)$.
G. Er verachtete die geistig armen S V O(2(3)1).
He despised the mentally deficient S V O(2(3)1).

CHAPTER 4.

Apposition I.

4. 1. Limits.

An appositive (by others termed an appositional) is placed within
square brackets [ ]; if it does not follow immediately after or before
the word it belongs to, stars (see **12**.3-5) are used.

It is not always easy to say where we have a simple junction and
where an apposition; in the former we have a closer connexion,
in the latter a looser coordination, which is often indicated by a
slight pause and by the intonation. Compare, for instance:
My friend Captain John Smith $1^2 1$ [111].
My brother Charles, the doctor $1^2 11[1]$.
My brother—Charles, the doctor $1^2 1$ [1] [1], thus with two appositions.

4. 2. Regular Cases of Apposition.

Edward VIII, the present King of England 12 [212(p1)].
Mr. Dimley, the president of the club, then rose S [12(p1)] 3 V.
I met Smith, one of my oldest friends S V O [1 p1($S^2 21$)].
The word 'love' 1 [1].

She presided with a grace all her own S V p1 [3S²2].
O my Amy, mine no more 21 [1²3ⁿ].
   (Given with others MEG II 15.6 as Semi-predicative post-adjuncts.)
F. Madame Massenet, née Lebrun, Dan. Fru Madsen, født Bruun
                                            11 [YP].
I like my tea very hot S V O(S²1) [32].
G. Ich trinke den kaffee gern warm S V O 3 [2].
   An apposition is often used to make clear how many and who are included in the plurals *we* and *you:*
You Germans admire Hitler; we English do not S [1] V O; S₂ [1] Vⁿ.

4. 3. With Prepositions.

The appositive may be a prepositional group (in the same way as the adjunct treated in **3**.4) :
Brown, never at a loss for an answer, replied S [3ⁿ p1 pO] V.

4. 4. Apposition with of.

In "some of us" as well as in "the City of London" *of* is justly called "partitive" : *some* and *the City* indicate a part of *us* and *London,* respectively. But we have another use of the preposition *of* which I have termed "appositional *of*" (*S.P.E.* Tract XXV, Oxford 1926) ; *of* is here simply a grammatical device to make it possible to join words which it is for some reason or other impossible or difficult idiomatically to join immediately. *A friend of mine* = 'a friend who is mine (my friend)', *the City of Rome* = 'the City which is Rome', etc. In the present symbols:
The City of Rome, the town of Sheffield 1 [p1].
No money of mine 2ᑫ1 [p1²].
He is no relation of ours S V P(2 1) [p1²].
The three of us 1 [p1].
That long nose of his 221 [p1²].
Little girls of eight years old 21 [p1(2ᑫ12)].
An old blackguard of a woman 21 [p1].
Her old sharper of a father 1²21 [p1].
F. Son coquin de frère 1²1 [p1].
It. Un amore di bimbo 1 [p1].
Sp. El bribon del criado 1 [p1].

Sp. El mamarracho de tu cuñado 'your funny little brother-in-law' 1 [p1($1^2$1)].

G. Ein alter schelm von lohnbedienter 21 [p1], note the nominative case.

Dan. Det bæst til Jensen 21 [p1].

Cf. also the Dan. expression Dit svin! 'you swine!'; Pg. seu burro! 'you ass' [1^2] 1, and the Sp. Pobrecitos de nosotros! P [pS]! or simply P S(p1)!

4.5. Note also the French appositions introduced with *que:* C'est une impertinence que cette histoire S* V P [3 21]* or s V P S(321).

Thus often with an infinitive: C'est un plaisir que de vous voir —and in the hardly analyzable: Ce que c'est que de nous!

Other examples of apposition see especially Ch. **12**.

CHAPTER 5.

Quantifiers.

5. 1. Adjectival.

On the theory of quantifiers see Comments, Ch. **32**.

Many friends, a few friends, some friends, four friends; G. Viele (wenige, einige, vier) freunde; F. Quelques amis; quatre amis 2^q1.

Much water, more water, enough water; G. Viel (mehr) wasser; Dan. Meget vand 2^q1.

Water enough; G. Wasser genug; Dan. Vand nok 12^q.

Very many friends 32^q1.

A great many friends $2(21)^q1$.

Many old friends $2^q1(21)$.

Much good white wine $2^q1(221)$.

I spent a good twenty minutes there S V O($2(3)2^q1$) 3.

Half (double) his money $2^q1(1^21)$.

The last few years $21(2^q1)$.

Those five boys came yesterday S(22^q1) V 3 (but: those five came yesterday S(21) V 3).

Much good has been done S(2^q1) V^b (but: much has been done S V^b).

5. 2. Substantival.

A dozen bottles 2ᑫ1.

G. Ein paar tage; Dan. Et par dage 2ᑫ1; note: die paar tage, de par dage.

G. Ein glas wasser; Dan. Et glas vand 2ᑫ1.

G. Ein glas guter wein 2ᑫ1(21).

5. 3. Genitival.

G. Eine flasche des edelsten weines 2ᑫ1(21).

L. Pars militum[1]; poculum vini 2ᑫ1.

L. Quid novi?; Ru. čto novago 2ᑫ?1.

G. Viele unserer freunde; eine anzahl dieser leute 2ᑫ1(21).

Ru. Stakan vina 'a glass of wine' 2ᑫ1.

Ru. Sto človĕk '100 men'; mnogo soldat 'many soldiers' 2ᑫ1.

　　In such combinations some would perhaps add (2) to 1 to denote the genitive case, cf. Comments **32**.3.

5. 4. With Prepositions.

A lot of money, plenty of money, a glass of water 2ᑫ1(p1).

A great deal of water 2(21)ᑫ1(p1).

F. Beaucoup de vin 2ᑫ1(p1).

F. Beaucoup plus de vin 32ᑫ1(p1).

A bottle of good wine 2ᑫ1(p21).

F. Une bouteille de vin rouge 2ᑫ1(p12).

Dozens of bottles 2ᑫ1(p1).

F. Rien de bon 2ᑫ1(p1).

One half of his money 2ᑫ1(p1(1^21)).

Very few of them arrived S(32ᑫ1(p1)) V.

Note (without *of*): Plenty more money, a lot more money 32ᑫ1.

CHAPTER 6.

Compounds.

6. 1. The Ordinary Type.

Railway; goldfish; bedroom; shipyard; headache; finger-ring; ring-finger; Sunday; the Burton case 2-1.

---

[1] If = 'one part of the soldiers', but if = 'the soldiers' portion' it is 11^2.

Westminster Abbey 2-1.

Railway refreshment room 2(2-1)-1(X-1).

An all-night club 2(2ᵍ1)-1.

Tiptoe; head-borough; It. capostazione; F. hôtel-Dieu; l'affaire Dreyfus; G. Sachsen-Weimar; Greek hippopotamos 1-2.

Everyday life 2(2-1)-1, or 2(21)1 if not regarded as a compound.

Sweet-shop; greenhouse; madhouse; lunatic asylum 2-1.

The unemployed problem 2-1.

South Wales 2-1, or 21.

New South Wales 2-2-1, or 21(2-1).

The South Welsh language 2(2-1)1.

Dead-letter office; first-class passenger 2(21)-1.

Three-storey house; ten-pound-note 2(2ᵍ1)-1.

G. Heiligegeiststrasse 2(21)-1.

A cat-and-dog life 2(1&1)-1.

Old-time steamboats 2(21)-1(2-1).

New Year Eve fancy dress ball 2(2(21)-1)-1(2(2-1)-1).

A snow-white dress; a colour-blind man 2(3-2)1.

Dan. To blå kjoler og tre snehvide 2ᵍ21 & 2ᵍ1(3-2).

A red-hot iron 2(2-2)1; a blue-green dress 2(3-2)1.

6. 2. Equipollent Compounds.

Sun-god; page-boy; fellow-citizen; queen-dowager; women-singers; pussy-cat; subject-matter, F. le roi-poète; femme poète 1-1.

Deaf-mutes 1-1; deaf-mute boys 2(2-2)1.

Austria-Hungary 1&°-1.

The Franco-Prussian war 2(2&°-2)1.

6. 3. Genitival compounds.

A ship's doctor 1²-1.

His new captain's uniform 1²21(1²-1).

Her warm mother's heart (*Mother's heart* a compound like G. *mutterherz*) 1²21(1²-1), different from the example above **3**.3 *his poor mother's heart* = 'the heart of his poor mother'.

A French lady's-maid 21(1²-1); *French* and *lady* stressed; *maid* unstressed. But a French lady's maid 1(21)²1; *lady* unstressed; *maid* stressed).

6. 4. Prepositions and Adverbs.

Father-in-law; F. Boîte aux lettres; chemin de fer; arc-en-ciel; moulin à vent 1-p1, or, which amounts to the same 1-2(p1).

Afterthought; Dan. Eftermæle; G. Nachgericht; Sp. antecámara 2(3)-1.

Foreword; Dan. forord; G. vorwort; F. avant-propos 2(3)-1.

Afternoon, F. Après-midi; G. Nachmittag; Dan. Eftermiddag p-1. Sp. anteojo p-1.

Afternoon tea 2(p-1)-1.

Afternoon excursion 2(p-1)-X.

Sunday afternoon concert 2(2(2-1)-1(p-1))-1.

West of England vulgarisms 2(1p1)-1.

A penny-in-the-slot machine 2(1p1)-1.

A house-to-house call; hand-to-hand fighting 2(p⁰1p1)-X or G.

Saturday-to-Monday parties 2(p⁰1p1)-1.

Maid-of-all-work 1-2(p1(21)).

F. Bonne à tout faire 1-2(OI).

G. Der vorletzte tag; F. L'avant-dernier jour 2(p-2)1.

An up-train; the under dog 3/2-1.

The maid's evening out 1²1(1-3).

There-on; Dan. Hertil; G. Dazu, darauf; F. Là-dessus 3(1-p).

6. 5. Adjuncts with Compounds.

An old clergyman; comfortable bachelor lodgings 21(2-1).

Here the adjunct qualifies the whole compound. It is differently in High churchmen; long-distance telephone; the dirty clothes-basket 2(21)-1.

New and second-hand bookseller 2(2 & 2(2+1)1)-1.

His big school-boy handwriting 1²22(2-1)1(2-1).·

G. Ein wilder schweinskopf, eine reitende artilleriekasserne

$$2*\ 1(2*-1)\ \text{or}\ 2(21)-1.$$

Dan. En optisk instrumentmager; unge dameportrætter; abstrakte videnskabsmænd 2* 1(2*-1) or 2(21)-1.

Many examples of this type are collected in MEG II 12.3 and Tanker og studier 159 ff. The inflexion of adjectives makes such combinations more conspicuous in German and Danish than in English. Hence also the star symbol.

A cold December night 21(2-1).

An early December night (i.e. early in D.) 2(2-1)-1 or 2(2 ᵐ1)-1.

6. 6. Adjunct + Substantive Compounds.

Compounds consisting of an adjective-adjunct and a substantive primary are denoted by the symbol +. Examples:

Blackbird; holiday; madman; Dan. gråvær (graavejr); F. beau-fils; petits-enfants; gentilhomme 2+1.

F. coffre-fort; vinaigre 1+2.

On the difference between these and *black bird, holiday* and, on the other hand, *sweetshop*, etc. see Comments **31**.8.

A first-rate second-hand bookshop 2(21)1(2(2+1)1)-1): *first-rate* (21) is secondary to the primary consisting of all the rest; *book* is primary to *second-hand* (2+1), and *second-hand book* is secondary to *shop*.

A sub-type is found in compounds of the type *red-coat*, Dan. *blåskæg; blue-stocking*, Dan. *blåstrømpe*, G. *blaustrumpf*, and with inverted order F. *bas-bleu*; the learned name for such compounds is *bahuvrihi*; some German linguists speak of *dick-kopfkomposita*.

The best way will be to take them as adjunct to a not-expressed primary:

Red-coat; Pur-sang 2(21)1⁰.

F. Bas-bleu; un Peau-Rouge 2(12)1⁰; cf. a bare-foot child 2(21)1; he walked barefoot S V 3(21).

6. 7. Blue-eyed.

A word like *blue-eyed* cannot be considered a compound of *blue* and *eyed*, but consists of the ordinary junction *blue eye* with the addition of a new element; this may be symbolized by adding the sign + after the junction:

A blue-eyed girl, a kindhearted woman, a good-natured man

$$2(21+)1.$$

Dan. En blåøjet pige; varmblodige dyr 2(21+)1.

G. Ein blauäugiges mädchen, warmblutige tiere 2(21+)1.

Common-sensible talk 2(21+)1.

In a similar way

A New Englander; practical joker; Pacific Islanders; natural philosophers; natural historians 1(21+).

Trade-unionism; gold medalist 1(2-1+).

6. 8. Dissolved Compound.

If the first part of a compound is treated as an ordinary adjunct, see MEG II, Ch. XIII, the symbol is (-).

Bosom friends 2(-)1.
Personal and party interests 2&2(-)1.
A small family hotel 21(2(-)1).
The evening and weekly papers 2(-)&21.
A Yorkshire young lady 2(-)1(21).
A purely family gathering 32(-)1.

6. 9. Isolated First Part.

The first part of a compound may in some cases be used for the whole (MEG II 8.9) :

A straw (=straw hat) ; a copper (=copper coin), soda (=soda water) $1(2\text{-}1^0)$.
We took returns (=return tickets) S V $O(2\text{-}1^0)$.
A buttonhole (=flower) $1(2(2\text{-}1)\text{-}1^0)$.
Dan. Diplomat (= d. frakke) $1(2\text{-}1^0)$; borgerdyden (=borgerdyds-skolen) $1(2(2\text{-}1)\text{-}1^0)$.
A twelfth-cake (short for twelfth-night cake) $2(2\text{-}1^0)\text{-}1$.

CHAPTER 7.

Independent Nexus.

7.1. A verbal sentence contains a verb in one of its finite forms, and may also contain one or more than one of the following items: a subject S, a direct object O, an indirect obj. *O,* a predicative P. Besides it may comprise one or more tertiary items 3. Such sentences constitute the ordinary type of sentences, though it would be wrong to consider them as the only "normal" or "normally constructed" sentences. We shall find other types of sentences in some of the following chapters, e.g. **9**.6, **13, 26.**
I live; he comes; it rains; Lat. Ego vivo; Petrus vivit; It. Io vivo; Pietro vive S V.
Lat. Vivit; It. Vive V, or S^0 V (Cf. on *vivo* **8**.1).
He takes a glass; G. Er nimmt ein glas; F. Il prend un verre S V O.
Ru. On vidit dom 'he sees the house' S V O; on ne vidit doma (genitive) S 3^n V O.
Ru. Brata ne bylo doma 'the brother (genitive) was not at home'
$$S\ 3^n\ V\ 3.$$

Ru. Net deneg 'there is no money' V^n S.

L. Miles vi utitur (medicina eget) S O V.

He eats very little meat S V $O(32^q1)$.

He eats very little; G. Er isst sehr wenig; F. Il mange très peu
$$S V O(2(3)1).$$

He despised the mentally deficient S V $O(2(3)1)$.

He puts on a cap S V 3 O.

He puts it on S V O 3.

He opens and shuts the door S $V(V \& V_2)$ O.

He takes his hat and stick S V $O(S^2 1) \& O_2(S^{20}1)$, or, if you
like, S V $O(S^2 1(1\&1_2))$.

Dan. Jeg minder dig om Dagen S V O p1; jeg mindes dagen
$$S V^{b/a} O.$$

F. (De l'argent.) J'en ai S O V.

F. J'ai assez d'argent S V $O(2^q1(p1))$.

F. J'en ai assez S O* V 2^{q*}.

F. (Le livre.) J'en ai lu quelques pages S 2* V $O*(2^q1)$.

7. 2. Indirect Object.

He gave her a dress; G. Er gab ihr ein kleid S V *O* O.

He gave it her S V *O* O.

G. Ich küsse ihr die hand S V *O* O.

F. Je lui serre la main; Sp. Yo le estrecho la mano S *O* V O.

G. Er entnimmt ihm alles; Dan. Han berøver ham alt S V *O* O.

F. Il lui prend tout S *O* V O.

F. Il me faut un nouveau pardessus S *O* V O(21).

F. Je lui croyais du talent S *O* V O.

F. Elle lui rappelait sa sœur S *O* V O (but: Dieu l'a rappelé à
lui S O V p1(=S)).

F. Il lui préfère son frère S *O* V $O(S^21)$.

F. Il me préfère à lui S O V p*O*.

F. Il nous en donne S *O* O V.

7. 3. Object of Result.

He makes (digs) a hole; he paints a portrait; G. Er bohrt ein loch;
er malt ein porträt; F. Il peint un portrait S V O^r.

She nodded her approval S V $O^r(S^2 X)$.

G. Er ärgerte sich die schwindsucht an den hals; Dan. Han ærgrede
sig en gulsot på halsen S V *O*(S) $O^r(S_2p1)$.

7. 4. Object or Tertiary?

She nodded her head; she clapped her hands S V O/3(S^2 1).
G. Wir laufen schlittschuh S V O/3.
It costs (us) five shillings S V (*O*) O/3(2^q1).
He struck her a heavy blow S V O O_2/3(21); cf. MEG III.14.

7. 5. Prepositional Group.

The combination of a preposition and its regimen may sometimes be used as a primary (subject or object):
From nine till twelve is three long hours S(p1p1) V P(2^q21).
You have till ten to-night S V O(p13).
F. Vous avez jusqu'à dix heures S V O(p1(2^q1)).
It cost him over thirty pounds; Dan. Det kostede ham over 50 kr.; G. Es kostete ihm über 50 mark S V *O* O(p1(2^q1))—which should probably be better symbolized ... O(2^q(p1)1).
F. Jusqu'aux enfants furent massacrés S(p1) O V^b.
G. An die tausend menschen waren versammelt S(p1(2^q1)) V P.
L. Ad duo milia et trecenti occisi sunt S(p2^q) V^b.
Sp. Hasta yo lo sé 'up to I (i.e. even I) know it' S(p1) O V.
Sp. Entre tú y yo lo pagaremos 'between us we shall pay' S(p1&1) O V

(note in these three the nominative).

We might place here:
To-day is Monday S(p1) V P.
We have all to-day to ourselves S V O(21(p1)) pS.

The so-called French "partitive article" is a case in point:
Il boit du vin; il a des amis S V O(p1).
Ce soir des amis vont arriver 3(21) S(p1) V.
Ceci est du vin S V P(p1).

But, *du, de la, des* often approaches a quantifying adjunct, and we might symbolize *du vin,* etc. 2^q1, cf. *avec du vin* p1(2^q1), and then
Il ne boit pas de vin S 3* V O(2^q*1).

CHAPTER 8.

Verbal Sentences Continued.

8. 1. Bracketing.

When two or more members of a sentence are denoted by one and the same word-form their symbols are joined by means of the brackets $\{\ \}$.

L. Amo puellam, It. amo la fanciulla $\{SV\}$ O.

Dan. Kom, G. komm, It. veni, F. viens! $\{SV\}$!

F. Sortons, It. usciamo! $\{SV\}$!

Magyar Látlak 'I see you', látjuk 'we see him' $\{SVO\}$.

Eskimo Takuvânga 'he sees me' $\{SVO\}$.

Finnish Purteni 'my boat', purtemme 'our boat' (nom.) $S\{1^21\}$.

Finnish purressamme 'in our boat' 3 $\{1^21\}$.

Cf. also the Finnish negative verbs, Comments **28**.5.
On the Portuguese bracketed infinitives see **15**.4.

8. 2. Reflexive.

He washes him; Dan. Han vasker ham S V O.
He washes himself; Dan. Han vasker sig S V O($=$S), or simply
$$S\ V\ O(S).$$
F. Il se lave S O(S) V.
He placed the boy behind him (Dan. bagved sig) S V O pl($=$S).
Tom takes his hat ($=$ John's, ejus); Dan. Tomas tar hans hat
$$S\ V\ O(1^21).$$
Tom takes his (own) hat; Dan. Tomas tar sin hat (suum)
$$S\ V\ O(S^21).$$
He gives himself airs; Dan. Han gir sig tid S V O(S) O.
Sp. El capitan se mató á si mismo S O(S) V pO(S2).
F. Le capitaine s'est tué lui-même S O(S) V [S2].
F. Je me permets une question S O(S) V O.
F. Elle s'est donnée à lui S O(S) V pO.
He talks with himself S V pl(S) or S W O(S).
He brought his brother with him S V O(S²1) pl(S).

It should be noted that this system of indicating reflexive pronouns covers both the English system with change according to

persons and added *self* (I ... myself, he ... himself), the Danish and
German with change of person and with a separate reflexive pronoun
in the third, but without 'self' (jeg ... mig, han ... sig; ich ... mich,
er ... sich), and the Russian system with the same reflexive pronoun
(ja ... sebja, on ... sebja). Similarly with possessives: the same
symbol is used for English (I ... my, he ... his, she ... her), Danish
(jeg ... min, han ... sin, hun ... sin), German (ich ... mein, er ...
sein, sie ... ihr), and Russian (ja ... svoj, on ... svoj, ona ... svoj).
On the manifold divergencies in well-known languages see PhilGr
220—225: our system expresses the underlying notions in the easiest
way.

In the well-known cases in which English dispenses with the reflexive object, we write, e.g.
I wash (shave), he washes (shaves) S V $O^0(S)$.

8. 3. Special Cases.

F. Il se souvient de cette affaire S O(S) V $pO_2(21)$.
F. Il s'en souvient S O(S) O_2 V.
G. Er nähert sich der stadt; Dan. Han nærmer sig byen
$$S V O(S) O_2.$$
F. Il s'approche de la ville S O(S) V pO_2.
G. Er zankt sich mit allen S V O(S) $p1 = S V O(S_x) pS_2$; cf. **8**.4.
F. Cela ne se dit pas S 3^* O(S) V $3^{n*} = S V^{bn}$.

With this should be compared It. *si* (**8**.8) and
G. Es fährt sich gut auf diesem wege S V O(S) 3 $p1(21)$.

8. 4. Reciprocal.

When we say, "Tom and John hate one another", the meaning
is "Tom hates John" and "John hates Tom". To express this cross-
wise relation, which of course is also found with more than two
subjects, I propose a small cross or x (to be read 'cross', not as the
letter) below the line:
They hate one another S V $O(S_x)$.
They took each other's hats S V $O(S_x{}^21)$.
They speak with one another; G. Sie reden miteinander S V pS_x.
F. Ils se haïssent S $O(S_x)$ V.
F. Ils s'entr'accusent les uns les autres S $O(S_x)$ V [SO].
G. Wir haben uns lange nicht gesehen S v $O(S_x)$ 3 3^n V.
The boys fight; we meet S V $O^0(S_x)$.

Dan. Drengene slås; vi mødes S $V^{b/a}$ $O^0(S_x)$, or S $\{VS_x\}$.

8. 5. Complex Verbal Phrases.

If we compare "he puts on a cap" (**7**.1) and "she waited on us", we discover an essential difference: in the first sentence *on* is an adverb and must be symbolized 3; if instead of "a cap" we take the pronoun *it, on* is placed after this. A similar change is impossible in the second sentence: *on* here is a preposition, and we may therefore symbolize S V p1. But a better analysis takes *waited on* as a whole, which has *us* as its object; the symbol for such a verbal complex is W. Note that it is possible to say in the passive: "We were waited on"; cf. also "He is difficult to deal with".

Look out for that cab! F. Prenez garde à cette voiture W O(21) ‼

He takes part in the conversation; F. Il prend part à la conversation;

G. Er nimmt teil an dem gespräch; Dan. Han tar del i samtalen

S W O.

G. Wir hoffen auf bessere tage; Dan. Vi håber på bedre tider

S W O(21).

G. Das geht über meinen verstand; Dan. Det går over min forstand

S W O($1^2$1).

G. Sie spotteten über seine ausdrücke; Dan. De gjorde nar av hans udtryk S W O($1^2$1).

F. Il se sert du couteau S W O, or, as in **8**.3, S O(S) V pO$_2$.

Dan. Jeg lagde mærke til stedet, fandt behag i stedet S W O.

He did away with himself S W O(S).

It is easy to see that there is a difference between

He is in love with Ann S W O,—and

He is in the garden with Ann S V 3(p1) 3(p1),

where *Ann* cannot on any account be considered the object as it can in the first sentence. In one case we ask: "What is he?", in the other "Where is he?"

He became aware of her; He was afraid of nothing

S W O = S V P (2p1).

Here we may perhaps place

F. Il jouit d'une bonne santé S W O(21), instead of S V p1(21).

There is a difficulty with the symbolization here proposed, namely that the phrase may sometimes be separated by an adverb: "She waited quietly on us"; why not write S W 3 O, even though this implies a slight infraction of our usual practice of following the text symbolized word for word; but, of course, S V* 3 p*O is also a clear notation; on the stars see **8**.6.

8. 6. Stars.

The signs * * serve to show that two (or more) items are to be understood together.

Evidence there was none S* 3/s V 2^q*.

L. Maximas tibi gratias ago 2* O O*$\left\{ SV \right\}$.

Jane's was a happy life S(1^{2}*) V P(21*). This construction is chiefly
    used to avoid the use of *one,* see MEG II. 10.9_8.

F. Ce livre-ci 2*13*.

G. Er sieht krank aus, Dan. Han ser syg ud S V* P 3*.

G. Das geht uns nichts an, Dan. Det kommer os ikke ved
$$S V* O 3^n 3*.$$

G. Wir wohnten der versammlung bei S V* O 3*.

What did they talk of? O*? v S V p*.

My state of mind 1^2* 1(1-p1*).

F. Il ne vient jamais S 3* V 3^n*.

F. Personne ne l'a vu S^n* 3* O V.

F. Il ne voit personne S 3* V O^n*.

F. Il n'a que dix francs S 3* V O(3*2^q1).

F. J'en ai lu le commencement S 2* V O*.

All men are not born to reign (Byron) S(2^q*1) V 3^n* P(YpI).

John told Robert's son that he must help him; the six possible
meanings may be written:

(a) S V O($1^2$1) O(3^c S V O(O)).
(b) S V O(1^{2}*1) O(3^c S V O*).
(c) S V O(1^{2}*1) O(3^c S_2* V O(S)).
(d) S V O(1^{2}*1) O(3^c S_2* V O(O)).
(e) S V O($1^2$1) O(3^c S_2(O) V O(S)).
(f) S V O(1^{2}*1) O(3^c S_2(O) V O*).

Here S always refers to John and O to Robert's son; but in order
to denote Robert himself stars must be employed.

Further examples of stars in various other chapters, e.g. **12, 23, 24**.

8. 7. Passive.

He was beaten by John S V^b pS^a.

A reward was offered the butler S V^b O, or, more circumstantially,
$$S(O^a) V^b O.$$

The butler was offered a reward S(O^a) V^b O.

The portrait was painted by Rembrandt S^r V^b pS^a.

We were waited on by Mary S W^b pS^a.

The doctor was sent for S W^b.

She was taken care of S W^b, or, more fully, S* W^b(V^{b}Op*).

The bed was not slept in S* V^{nb} p*.

G. Es wird getanzt S V^b.

Sw. Det kämpades från morgon till kväll S V^b p1 p1.

The book sells well; the material washes easily S V$^{a/b}$ 3.

8. 8. O/S.

What ails Tom? S/O? V O/S.

    (The old "What aileth thee?" has become „What ailst thou?")

G. Mich friert; mir graut O/S V.

G. Mich jammert seiner O/S V 3/O.

L. Pudet eum sceleris V O/S 3/O.

G. Mich reut dieser tat O/S V 3/O(21).

F. Me voici O/S $\left\{ \text{V3} \right\}$.

It. Eccolo $\left\{ \text{3 O/S} \right\}$.

It. Questo non si dice S/O 3^n O/S V.

It. Si vende carne; Si vendono biglietti O/S V S/O.

By a shifting (see PhilGr 161) this leads to Si viene S V; Si vende biglietti S V O, in which *si* must be considered S with the same generic signification as F. *on*. Cf. above on F. Cela ne se dit pas.

Sp. Se le trató como á un rey 'on l'a traité comme un roi'

                         S/O O V 3^c p1.

Sp. Se conoce al verdadero amigo en la necesidad S/O V pO(21) pl.

Dan. Mig synes du har ret (= G. Mir scheint, du hast recht)

    O V S(S$_2$ V O$_2$) has become: Jeg synes du har ret

                         S V O (S$_2$ V O$_2$).

8. 9. Lesser Subject.

G. Es kamen zwei junge leute s V S(2^{q}21).

G. Es irrt der mensch, so lange er strebt s V S 3(3^{cc} S V).

F. Il est arrivé un grand malheur s V S(21).

Sw. Det fanns många skepp; Det hade fallit mycket snö s V S(2^{q}1).

It is a long way to Tipperary s V S(21 p1), or S V P(21) p1.

Dan. Det må vente med betalingen s V pS; Det er smått med fortjenesten s V P pS.

F. Il naît dans ce village cent enfants par an s V p1(21) S(2^{q}1) pl.

    Other examples of s are found in the chapters on Infinitive **(17, 18)**, Gerund (**19**), and Clauses (**22** ff.).

CHAPTER 9.

Predicative.

9. 1. Ordinary.

The symbol is P. It must be emphasized that this is different from *Predicate*—the term used ordinarily for the whole of a (normally constructed) sentence minus the subject. It may be doubtful whether the bipartition of a sentence into Subject and Predicate found in most books on the theory of grammar has any great value : anyhow there is no need to create a symbol for predicate in that sense. What is meant here by *predicative* will appear from the examples, see also the discussion below Ch. **35**. The term is taken in a wider sense than in most of the books that make use of it, see especially **9**.4 and **9**.5. (French grammarians generally say *attribut*).
She is an actress ; F. Elle est actrice ; G. Sie ist schauspielerin S V P.
He is (seems, looks) angry ; he proved innocent S V P.
She is young and pretty S V P & P_2.
He is a little fool S V P(21) ; He is a little mad S V P(32) ; cf. Dan.
Han er en lille nar, han er lidt gal ; G. Er ist ein kleiner narr, er ist ein bischen toll ; F. Il est un petit fou, il est un peu fou.
The soup is warm enough ; Dan. Suppen er varm nok S V P(23).
She is ten years old ; The box is two feet long S V P(3(2^q1)2).
This is not good S V^n P(2).
This is no good S V P(2^q1).
He was not himself that night ; Dan. Han var ikke sig selv den aften
S V^n P(S) 3(21) ; cf. **8**.3.
F. Elle a l'air intelligente S W P.
Ru. On byl soldat 'he was a soldier' (permanently) S V P.
Ru. On byl togda soldatom 'he was then a soldier' (for the time being) S V 3 P.
Ru. On okazalsa nevinnym 'he proved (to be) innocent' S V P.
Fi. Isäni on kipeä 'my father is ill' (permanently) S V P.
Fi. Isäni on kipeänä 'my father is ill' (for the moment) S V P.

9. 2. Predicative of Result.

He gets (becomes, grows) angry S V P^r.
He fell ill ; G. Er wurde krank ; F. Il tomba malade S V P^r.
The milk turns sour ; The dream came true ; The fire burns low
S V P^r.
L. Cicero consul fit S P^r V.

Fi. Isäni on jo tullut kipeäksi 'my father has fallen ill' S V Pr.
"Predicatives of becoming" (MEG III. 18) are thus treated like
"objects of result".

9. 3. Adverbs and Prepositional Groups.

The rain is over; G. Der regen ist vorüber S V P(3).
The war is at an end; she is with child; G. Er ist ausser atem;
Dan. Han er fra forstanden S V P(p1).
She looked a little out of health S V P(3pp1).
F. Je suis d'un autre avis S V P(p1(21)).
He was in love with her S V P(p1) 3(p1), or S W O; cf. **8**.5.
He fell in love with her S V Pr(p1) 3(p1), or S W O.
He came of age last year S V Pr(p1) 3(21).
It is two (o'clock) S V P; F. Il est deux heures S V P(2^q1) — but
should the corresponding Sp. Son las dos—be written V S or
V P (with S^0)?
The apple is far from ripe; Dan. Æblet er langtfra modent

S V P(3p2).

On the predicative with a passive verb see Ch. **16**.

9. 4. Subjunct-Predicatives.
(Cf. MEG III 18.7.)

Her eyes are the same colour as mine S(1^21) V P(21) 3c 1.
What age is he? P(2? 1) V S.
He is twenty S V P(1^q) = He is twenty years S V P(2^q1) = He is
twenty years old S V P(3(2^q1)2).
The bishop was high-church S V P(2+1).
She turned lead-colour S V Pr(2-1).
L. Animo meliore sunt gladiatores P(12) V S.
L. Natura humana aevi brevis est S(12) P(12)² V.
G. Der mann war guten mutes, (guter dinge; einer anderen ansicht)

S V P(21)².

9. 5. Predicative after a Particle (Preposition).
(Cf. PhilGr 132, MEG IV, ch. 23).

He lived as a saint; G. Er lebte als junggeselle; F. Il vivait comme
un saint S V pP. Cf. **12**.5.
F. Il a agi en homme consciencieux S* V p1(P*(12)).

F. Il nous traite de fripons S O* V pP*.

F. Je le tiens pour fou S O* V pP*.

It. Meglio vivere un giorno da leone che cent' anni da pecora (Mussolini) P S(I 3 pP$_2$) 3^c 3 (2^{q}1) pP$_3$.

They were changed from men to swine; Dan. De blev forvandlede fra mennesker til svin S V^b pP pP$_2$^{r}.
(The role of the preposition is evidently different from that in "He flew from London to Paris").

G. Sie ernannten ihn zum regierungsrat; Dan. De udnævnte ham til etatsråd; G. Er nimmt Anna zur frau S V O pP^r.

G. Er gilt für ein genie S V pP.

Her temperature had dropped to normal S(1^{2}1) V pP^r.

She had grown into a tall girl; The town had shrunk into a small hamlet S V pP^r(21).

Dan. En lille fjer blev til fem høns S(21) V pP^r(2^{q}1).

F. De royaliste qu'il était, il est devenu socialiste p12(P^{c}SV) S V P^r.

9. 6. Predicatives without a Verb (without a 'Copula'):

Ru. On soldat 'he (is) a soldier'; ja bolen 'I (am) ill'; dom nov 'the house (is) new' S P; but: dom novyj 'a (the) new house'
12.

Sorry! My mistake ! P ! or P S^0 !

Splendid!; G. Grossartig!; Dan. Udmærket!; Nonsense!; G. Unsinn!; Dan. Sludder! P!

All right! S P—but: That is all right S V P(32).

Quite serious, all this P(32) S(21).

Gk. Ouk agathon polukoiranie P(3^{n}2) S.

F. Charmante, la petite Pauline! P S(21).

Dan. Godt det samme P S.

All haile Macbeth!; G. Heil Hitler! P S!!

L. Beati possidentes P S.

L. Praesens imperfectum, perfectum futurum S P P$_2$ S$_2$.

L. Summum jus summa injuria S(21) P(21).

Better go at once P S(I 3).

F. Inutile de raisonner sur la mort P S(Ip1).

Dan. Folkets kærlighed min styrke S(S$_2$^{2}X) P(S$_3$^{2}X).

Smoking prohibited S(G) P(Y^b).

It. Peccato celato mezzo perdonato S(12(Y)) P(32(Y^b)).

What a pity that he should die so soon P(2!1) S(3^c S$_2$V 3) =
G. Schade, dass er so früh sterben sollte P S(3^c S$_2$ 3V) =

F. Quel dommage qu'il soit mort si tôt P(2!1) S(3ᶜ S₂V3).
See many similar examples PhilGr 121 ff.
Better late than never P S(3) 3ᶜ S₂(3).

9. 7. O/P.

She will make a good wife; F. Elle fera une bonne ménagère
$$S \ V \ O/P(21).$$
F. Il fait froid S V O/P.
Sp. Hace frio; It. Fa freddo V O/P.
F. Il fait cher vivre à Paris s V O/P S(Ip1).

9. 8. No Predicative.

Is he rich? Yes, he is V S P? Z, S V P⁰.
On predicatives in a dependent nexus see Ch. **14.**

CHAPTER 10.

Tertiaries, etc.

10. 1. Tertiaries.

Examples are found here and there in other chapters, e.g. **3**.1.
He arrived there yesterday S V 3 3₂ or simply S V 3 3.
He arrived last night, F. Il est arrivé ce soir S V 3(21).
F. J'en suis surpris S 3 V.
F. Je n'y vois rien S 3* 3 V Oⁿ*.
I feel a great deal better S V P(3(21)q2).
I don't care twopence about it S Vⁿ 3(2q1) p1.
We talked face to face S V 3(1p1).
No doubt, the meeting will be a great success 3(21) S V P(21).
They fought tooth and nail S V 3(1&1).
He comes here every now and then S V 3 3(21(3&3)).
New-laid eggs; newly appointed ministers 3 2(Y) 1.
Can you spare me a few minutes? (a) v S V O O? (b) v S V O 3?
    The example is taken from Maria Schubiger "The Role of In-
tonation" (St. Gallen 1935, p. 16: in (a) *a few minutes,* in (b) the
verb has the "intonation turn". In (a) the meaning is "Can you
give me a few minutes of your time?", in (b) "Will you excuse my
absence for a few minutes?" (*A few minutes* if analyzed = 2q1).

Here goes! 3 V.

Christmas last year was jolly S 3(21) V P, or S(12(21)) V P.

He came a month ago S V 3(1p), or S V 3(S₂P).

F. Il est venu il y a un mois S V 3(S₂ 3 V O).

<h2 align="center">10. 2. Quaternaries, etc.</h2>

He plays very well, F. Il joue très bien, G. Er spielt sehr gut S V 43.

He will learn it soon enough S V O 34.

This happened long before the war, F. Ça est arrivé longtemps avant
la guerre S V 43(p1).

He was usually well-dressed S V 3 P(3Y^b).

He was unusually well-dressed S V P(43Y^b).

He came somewhat later, G. Er kam etwas später S V 43.

You walk far too rapidly S V 543.

They march four deep S V 4q3, or, if *deep* is taken as P: S V P(3q2).

I bought it second-hand and very cheap S V O 3(2+1) & 43.

How much more comfortably are things arranged now

6!543 V S P(Y^b) 3

(or *how much* together 5!).

<h2 align="center">10. 3. Prepositional Groups.</h2>

The combination of a preposition and the words it governs (its
object as it is often called) is one of the most frequent forms of
tertiaries; it is not, however, necessary to indicate expressly that
such a group is a tertiary; the word governed by a preposition is a
primary (except in some of the cases mentioned in **9**.5).

I found John in the garden; G. Ich traf Hans im garten; F. J'ai
trouvé Jean dans le jardin S V O p1 (=3(p1)).

Composite prepositions are denoted pp:

He stopped on account of the noise; F. Il a cessé à cause du bruit

S V pp1.

He started from here at ten S V p1 p1.

Note. On prepositional groups as S or O see **7**.5; as P see **9**.3.
A group p1 may also be a secondary and must then be written 2(p1),
see **3**.4. As a primary such a group functions also when it is itself
governed by a preposition, see MEG III.1.2:

Since before the war; from under the table; Sp. De entre los cuer-
nos; Du. Van onder de tafel p1(p1).

F. Avec des amis p1(p1) ; cf. on the "partitive article" **7**.5.
He has been here for well over a month S V 3 p1(4p1).

10. 4. Place of Preposition.

The preposition does not always stand before its regimen :
All the world over; Dan. Hele verden over 1(21)p.
G. Das tal entlang; Ihm gegenüber; L. Capulo tenus; mecum 1p.
G. Er läuft ihr nach S V 1p, which approaches S V* O 3*.

The preposition may be removed from its regimen; in this case
stars must be used to show their connexion :
What are you talking of? 1?* v S V p*.
Dan. Hvad taler I om? 1?* V S p*.
Dan. Det tar jeg mig ikke av 1* V S O(S) 3^n p*.
Other examples in Clauses, see Ch. **23**.

10. 5. 3/s.

There are many churches there; Dan. Der er mange kirker der
    (dær) ; Du. Er zijn vele kerken daar 3/s V S(2^{q}1) 3.
How much truth is there in that statement? S(3?2^{q}1) V 3/s p1.
There comes an end to all things 3/s V S p1(21).
Du. Er wordt geklopt; Dan. Der danses 3/s V^b.
Du. Er zullen geschenken uitgedeeld worden 3/s v S V^b.
Dan. Der skal uddeles gaver 3/s V^b S.
There is nothing very serious the matter 3/s V S(132) P.
There is nothing good left 3/s V S(12) P.
Dan. Der kan ingen finde det; Der har een gjort ulykker

3/s v S V O.

CHAPTER 11.

Recipient.

11. 1. R.

The symbol R is used (somewhat vaguely) for something that is
governed by some word that is not a verb or a verbid (I,G,X, or Y)
in about the same way as an object is governed by any of these.
The ring is worth 5 pounds S V P(2R(2^{q}1)).
A ring worth 5 pounds 12R(2^{q}1).

G. Der ring ist 50 mark wert; Dan. Ringen er 50 kr. værd; G. Die strecke ist 50 meter lang S V P(R(2^q1)2).

He is like his father S V P(2R(S^21)).

G. Er ist seinem vater ähnlich; Dan. Han er sin far lig

$$S \ V \ P(R(S^21)2).$$

Dan. Han blev hende var S V P^r(R2).

G. Seid ihr mich schon müde? V S R* 3 P* ?

11. 2. Dative of Various Languages.

In most cases R stands for the dative in French, etc. Its use resembles that of *O,* but the latter symbol is used only where there is in the same sentence a direct beside the indirect object.

F. Il lui était impossible de répondre s R V P S(I).

G. Es war ihm unmöglich zu antworten, Dan. Det var ham umuligt at svare s V R P S(I).

Sp. Le era imposible de responder R V P S(I).

Ru. Emu nevozmožno otvěčat' R P S(I).

F. Cela m'est désagréable S R V P.

G. Das ist mir unangenehm; Dan. Det er mig ubehageligt S V R P.

G. Ein mir unangenehmer auftrag; Dan. Et mig ubehageligt hverv

$$R \ 2 \ 1.$$

Dan. Det er mig en stor ære S V P(R21).

G. Mir ist er tot R V S P.

G. Das ist mir zu teuer; Dan. Det er mig for dyrt S V R P(32).

11. 3. Continued.

G. Er lebt nur seiner familie S V 3 R(S^21).

L. Non tibi ipsi sed toti reipublicae vivis 3^n R(12) & R_2(21)$\left\{ SV \right\}$.

F. Il me vient une idée s R V S.

F. Peu m'importe 3 R V S^0.

Dan. Peter var sin far en dyr søn; G. Peter war seinem vater ein teurer sohn S V R(S^21) P(21).

Ru. On mně drug 'he is a friend of mine (to me)' S R P.

Ru. Skol'ko vam lět? 'How much to you of years? = How old are you?' 2^q*? R 1*.

Ru. Vam sdavat' 'you are to deal' R S(I).

Ru. Vot vam na čaj 'here for you for tea, i.e. a tip' 3 R pl S^0.

L. Hoc mihi est faciendum S R V P(Y^b).

L. Mihi est propositum in taberna mori R V P S(plI).

11. 4. **Final Examples.**

G. Er schlug ihm auf die schulter S V R* p1*.

(but Er schlug ihn auf die schulter S V O p1).

G. Er fiel ihm um den hals; Dan. Han faldt ham om halsen

S V R p1.

G. Das herz klopft mir; Die hände zittern mir S V R.

It. Di piacere mi balza il cuor p1 R V S.

G. Gott sei dank! R V S!!

Dan. Ære være gud! S V R!!

L. Soli deo gloria! R(21) S!!

Ru. Zemlja emu përyško! '(May) the earth (be) to him a feather!'

S R P!!

G. Dem ist nicht so R V 3^n P.

CHAPTER 12.

Extraposition and Apposition.

12. 1. Extraposition.

Closely related to apposition, of which we gave examples in Chapter **4,** is extraposition; a word, or a group of words, is placed, as it were, outside the sentence as if it had nothing to do there. This is often in speech marked by means of a pause, in writing, by a comma or a dash, though sometimes a semicolon or a full stop is used.

Zionism—what is that to me? [1*] P? V S* p1.

The rain it raineth every day [1] S V 3(21).

The man who is coming there, do you know his name?

[12(S^{c}V3)]* v S V O(1²*1)?

F. La dame qui vient d'entrer, la connais-tu? [12(S^{c}V)] O V S?

G. Die sterne, die begehrt man nicht [1] O V S 3^n.

G. Das pergament, ist das der heil'ge brunnen? [1*] V S* P(21)?

It. I piccoli debiti bisogna pagarli [21]* V I O*.

Gr. Hos ho men entha katheude polutlas dios Odusseus

3 S* 33 V [221*].

What the devil do you want? O? [1] v S V.

Prepositional groups in extraposition:

As to an Abyssinian victory, that is out of the question

pp1(21) S V P(pp1).

F. Quant à l'opinion de ces messieurs, je m'en fiche
$$[pp1*2(p1)] \ S \ O(S) \ O_2* \ V.$$

12. 2. Transition to Predicative.

There he sat, a giant among dwarfs 3 S V [1 p1].
I discovered Mont Blanc, that giant among mountains
$$S \ V \ O \ [21p1].$$

In MEG III 17.1 a whole series of examples has been given, in which from such cases of "extraposition" we are led through "apposition" and "quasi-predicatives" to real predicatives without any sharp lines of demarcation. Here I shall select from these a few cases which might be analyzed either way:
He married young and died poor S V [2] & V_2[2], or S V P & V_2 P_2.
The natives go naked S V [2], or S V P.

"In sentences with quasi-predicatives the nexus is wholly or nearly complete without the quasi-predicative; in sentences with real predicatives it is not; and in the sentences containing the verb *be* the real nexus is between the subject and the predicative, as *be* is a negligible factor from the notional point of view." (MEG).

12. 3. Sentences with Apposition.

I met Lawrence, the novelist, not the Colonel S V O [1] [3ⁿ 1].
It is all over now S* V [2*] P 3.
It was Sunday, always a dull day in London S V P [3 21 p1].
He had a shilling a week pocket money S V O(1 3 [2-1]).
They were themselves busy that day S* V [1*] P 3(21).
She had her son with her, Robert by name S V O*(S²1) pS [1* p1].

12. 4. Special Cases.

Ill though (or, as) he was, he received us [P 3ᶜ S V] S V O.
He despised the Church, whether high or low S V O [2 & 2].
His last night alive 1²* 21 [2*].

In Carlyle's sentence
Alive they should not take him, not they alive him alive—the first *alive* is clearly in apposition, but to what? I symbolize:
[2] S Vⁿ O 3ⁿ S[2] O[2].
Their first talks alone together on the balcony S²*2X [23 p1]*.
Sp. Teneis los Españoles una lengua hermosa 'you Spanish have a
fine language' $\left\{ S*V \right\}$ [S*] O(12).

Sp. Mas me quiero ir Sancho a cielo que gobernador al infierno

$$3 \ O \left\{ SV \right\} O(I \ [1] \ p1) \ 3^c \ [1] \ p1.$$

L. Quisque suos patimur manes [S] $2^* \left\{ \ SV \ \right\} O^*.$

F. Son père à lui $1^{2*}1$ [p1*].

Sp. Su libre de usted $1^{2*}1$ [p1*]

F. Il me le donne à moi S O^* O V [p1*].

G. Dem herrn sein hut; Dan. dial. E kuon hinner hat; Du. Vondel
z'n gedichten [R*] $1^{*2}1$.

G. Von den kraftwagen ist dem Wilhelm seiner der beste

$$p1 \ V \ S([R^*] \ 1^{*2}1^\circ) \ P.$$

12. 5. As.

As (a particle-preposition with a predicative) is often found in
an appositive, cf. **9**.5 :

He was quite happy as a bachelor S* V P(32) [pP*].

His decisions as a judge S^{2*} X [pP*].

This of course applies to one use only of the many-sided word *as*.
Cf. **23**.5 and p. 71.

12. 6. Restrictive Apposition.

Generally what is within the square brackets is identical with the
item it stands in opposition to; thus in

We were all very happy S* V [2*] P(32).

But in the following cases the extent of the two is not the same :

We were many of us very happy S* V $[1^q$ p1]* P(32).

I saw the soldiers, some of them very young indeed

$$S \ V \ O \ [1^q p1 \ 323].$$

The boys got a shilling each S* V O [1*].

He gave the boys a shilling each S V O^* O [1*].

I paid 6d. each for these cigars S V O [1] p1(21).

An apposition may even really cancel the meaning of the first
word :

We were none of us very happy S* V [1p1]* P(32).

12. 7. Vocative.

What is traditionally termed a 'vocative' may, if the sentence
contains an expressed or implied *you,* be said to be in apposition
to this, as in :

I am talking of you, John S V p1 [1].

Come here at once, Mary! $\left\{ S*V \right\}$ 3 3 [1*]❗

But very often there is no *you* implied except in the name of the person or persons addressed; then the 'vocative' stands in extraposition: our symbol [ ] covers extraposition as well as apposition. This is not true, John S V^n P [1].

In some languages, but not in the modern West-European languages, the vocative is a special case.

12. 8. A whole Idea.

A substantive may stand in apposition to the idea contained in a verb, or rather to the whole idea contained in the sentence; we may for such cases use the symbol § and show by its place whether it refers to what precedes or what follows:

I want a hero—an uncommon want (Byron) S V O [§2X].

I read the Times first thing in the morning S V O [§21p1].

Similar cases are the following:

Her voice was euer soft, Gentle, and low, an excellent thing in woman (Sh) $S(1^21)$ V 3 $P(2\&{}^02\&2)$ [§ 21 p1].

He was playing with the children, an unusual thing in those days

S V p1 [§21p1(21)].

F. ... et, chose curieuse, il est parti sans un mot & [12§] S V p1.

Needless to say, we regret this [PS(I)§] S_2 V O.

Cf. Relative clauses and Speaker's aside, Ch. **25**.

CHAPTER 13.

Various Kinds of Sentences.

13. 1. Request.

(Injunction, command, summons, entreaty, prayer).

Symbol: ❗ (heavy type); in writing the mark of exclamation is underlined doubly.

Note that the symbol for ordinary exclamations is the usual type ! (see **13**.5).

Come at once! $\left\{ SV \right\}_3$ ❗, or S^0 V 3 ❗

F. Viens de suite! G. Komm sofort! $\left\{ SV \right\}$ 3 ❗

F. Sortons! $\left\{ SV \right\}$ ❗
Don't you stir! v^n S V ❗

L. Mihi crede! O $\{SV\}$!
Now! Out! 3!
Out with you! 3 pS!
John! [if = Come here, John!] S!
One moment! 2^q1!
Silence! X!
G.Abfahrt!; = It. Partenza! X!
G. Vorsicht! Sp. Cuidado! X! = With care! pX! = Dan. For-
  sigtig! P! = It. Posa piano! V 3!
G. Nicht hinauslehnen! 3^n I!
It. Tenere la destra I O!
(Waiter,) matches! 1!
Another bottle, please! 21 V!
Just one moment! 32^q1!
Not a word of this to anyone! 3^n 21 p1 p1!
Dan. Ikke mine ord igen! 3^n $1^2$1 3!
Eyes right! G. Augen rechts! 13!
God, bless the King! 1! V O!
G. Gehen wir! V S!
Let us (Let's) go!; Dan. Lad os gå! V O(S I)!
Du. Laten we maar gaan! V O(S 3 I)!
  In these it would be possible to write v S V!
Let the dead bury their dead! V O(SIO$_2$(S^{2}1))!
Let us go! (if = 'allow us to go')$\{SV\}$ O O(I)!

13. 2. Question.

Questions are a kind of requests—requests to the hearer to give information or to resolve the doubt of the speaker on a certain point. We give first cases in which the question-mark is placed after the whole sentence.
Tom? [e.g. = Did Tom do it?] S ?
  [e.g. = Did you see Tom?] O ?
Alone? [e.g. = Are you alone?] P ?
Here? 3 ?
Is he ill? V S P ?
G. Kam er? Dan. Kom han? V S ?
Dan. Mon han kom? 3 S V ?
Did he come? Has he come? Will he come? F. Est-il venu? Va-t-il
  venir? G. Ist er gekommen? Wird er kommen? v S V ?

F. Ton ami est-il venu? S(1²1) v s V ?

Ru. Živ li ešcë vaš brat? 'is your brother still alive?' P 3 3 S(1²1) ?

Ru. Est' li u vas den'gi? 'Is (there) with you money, have you got any money' V 3 p1 S ?

13. 3. Special Questions.

Next cases in which the question is centred on one particular interrogative word, which then must have the mark affixed to it ("x-questions").

Who said it? G. Wer sagte das? S? V O.

Whom are you talking of? 1*? v S V p*.

What has he? G. Was sagte er? O? V S.

What did he say? Whom did he see? O? v S V.

What is he? P? V S.

What (which) boy said it? S(2? 1) V O.

What age person is she? P(2(2?1)-1) V S.

Whose daughter is she? G. Wessen tochter ist sie? P(1²? 1) V S.

When (Where, How) was it? G. Wann (Wo, Wie) war es? 3? V S.

Where does he come from? 3?* v S V p*.

How big is he? G. Wie gross ist er? P(3? 2) V S.

How often does he come? 3?(43) v S V.

How many children has he? O(2�q?(32)1) V S.

What to do? O? I.

Why not go at once? 3? 3ⁿ I 3.

Who is who? S? V P?

F. Qui l'a dit? S? O V.

F. Qu'a-t-il dit? O? v S V.

F. Qu'importe? 3? V or 3? V S⁰.

F. De quoi parlez-vous? p1? V S.

F. D'où vient-il? p1? V S.

F. Combien a-t-il d'enfants? 2�q*? V S p1*.

F. Quel âge avez-vous? O(2?1) V S.

Dan. Hvor mon han er? 3? 3 S V.

13. 4. Request in form of a question?/!

Will you take that chair? v S V O(21) ?/!

Won't you do me that service? vⁿ S V *O* O(21) ?/!

F. Voulez-vous bien entendre? G. Wollen Sie gefälligst hören?

v S 3 V ?/!

13. 5. Exclamation (Wonder, Emotion generally).

Denoted by the simple exclamation point.

How dreadful! 3! P, or, more fully, 3! P S⁰.

What a nuisance! P(2!1), or the same with S⁰.

What an ass he is P(2!1) S V.

You fool! SP !

The pity of it! XpS !

How kind of you to come! P(3!2) p1(S₂*) S(I*).

How people can be such fools! 3! S V P(21).

How late you are! P(3!2) S V.

G. Wie spät Sie kommen! 4!3 S V.

I blush to think of what fools we were S V pI p1(P(2!1)SV).

Let them talk! V O(SI) ! = F. Qu'ils parlent! 3ᶜ S V !

    (Thus with ! instead of ! as above **13.**1).

Good Gracious! is he dead? 21 ! V S P ?

13. 6. Wish.

Wish denoted by double exclamation point.

God bless the King! S V O !!

Grammar be hanged! S Vᵇ !!

May you be happy! v S V P !!

G. Es lebe der führer! s V S !!

F. Vive la liberté! V S !!

F. A bas les dictateurs! 3 S !!

G. Möchte er doch kommen! v S 3 V !!

Could we but trust Germany! v S 3 V O !!

Had you only been here! v S 3 V 3 !!

Dan. Bare (gid) han kom! 3 S V !!

Dan. Hvem der var rig! S s V P !!

If only I had a true friend! F. Si seulement j'avais un véritable ami!

    Dan. Hvis bare jeg havde en sand ven! 3ᶜᶜ S V O(21) !!

L. Utinam Clodius viveret! 3 S V !!

F. Au revoir! G. Auf wiedersehen! pI !!

It. A rivederla p1(IO) !!

Dan. På gensyn! Ru. Do svidanija! pX !!

CHAPTER 14.

Dependent Nexus (Nominal).

14. 1. Object.

I considered this a lie S V O(S_2P).
He found the bird flown S V O(S_2P).
He proved himself a fine fellow S V O(SP(21)).
She wishes the dinner at an end S V O^r(S_2P(p1)).
Dan. Jeg ønsker varerne bragt hjem S V O^r(S_2Y^{b}3).
They made him president; He painted the door red S V O^r(S_2P).
He slept himself sober S V O^r(SP).
Dan. Han drak sig fuld S V O^r(SP).
Han drak ham fuld S V O^r(S_2P).
G. Er läuft die füsse wund; Man schlug ihn tot S V O^r(S_2P).
G. Sie weinte sich die augen rot S V O(S) O^r(S_2P).
She screamed herself into a fit; G. Er lief sich ausser atem
$$S V O^r(SP(p1)).$$
Practice makes perfect S(X) V O^r($S_2{}^0$P).
Dan. Jeg gjorde opmærksom på fejlen S V O^r($S_2{}^0$ P p1).

14. 2. Junction Virtually Nexus.

Too many cooks spoil the broth S(3PS_2) V O; see MEG III 11.1$_2$.
    The meaning is 'the fact that the cooks are too many, etc.' .
(But: Too many cooks are dirty S(32^{q}1) V P.)
No news is good news S(PS_2) V P(21).
You must put up with no hot dinner S W O(PS_2(21)).
    In the last two examples *no* should perhaps be transcribed P(2^q).[1]

14. 3. Various Instances.

F. On célébra Rocroi délivré S V O(S_2P(Y)).
F. Le verrou poussé l'avait surprise S(S_2P(Y)) O V.
It is a load off my mind S V P(S_2P$_2$(p1)).
It was a disagreeable duty over S V P(S_2(21)P$_2$).
That might mean another job gone S V O(S_2(21)P).

---

[1] A somewhat similar case is found in Dante's "Nessun maggior dolore Che ricordarsi del tempo felice Nella miseria", which means "Nessun dolore è maggiore ..." (or "Non si trova nessun maggiore dolore che...").

14. 4. Nexus after a Preposition.

I slept with the windows open S V p1(S_2P).
She sat with the colour gone from her face S V p1(S_2P(Yp1($S^2$1))).
Dan. Han kom hjem med hænderne tomme S V 3 p1(S_2P).
I was happier with her away S V P p1(S_2P_2).
After Eve seduced; L. Post urbem conditam p1(SP).
It. Dopo fatta la correzione; Sp. Despues de escrito el libro p1(PS).
He wished her joy on a rival gone S V *O* O p1(S_2P).
They came back with Jones as spokesman S V 3 p1(S_2pP); cf. **9**.5.

14. 5. Nexus Tertiary.

Dinner over, we played bridge 3(SP) S_2 V O, or, better, in spite
    of the order, with *we* as the principal subject 3(S_2P) S V O.
This done, he bade us good-night 3(S_2P) S V *O* O.
Weather permitting we start to-morrow 3(S_2P(Y)) S V 3.
He stood hat in hand S V 3(S_2P(p1)).
You cannot expect more, prices being what they are
                 S V^n O 3(S_2P(YP_2($P^c S_2$V))).
There being no taxis, I walked 3(3/s P(Y)S_2(2^q1)) S V.
L. Augustus natus est Cicerone consule S V 3(S_2P).
L. Libro completo, saltat auctor pede laeto 3(S_2P(Y^b)) V S 3(12).
F. Ces dispositions prises, il mourut 3(S_2(21)P) S V.
F. Morte la bête, mort le venin 3(PS_2) P S.
It. Morto il padre egli andò a Roma 3(PS_2) S V p1.
G. Louise kommt zurück, einen mantel umgeworfen S V 3 3(S_2P).
G. Unverrichteter dinge kam er zurück 3(PS_2) V S 3.
Dan. Alt vel overvejet, rejser jeg imorgen 3($S_2$3P) V S 3.
Sp. Rosario no se opondrá, queriendolo yo S 3^n O V 3(POS_2).

CHAPTER 15.

Dependent Infinitival Nexus.

15. 1. Object.

We saw him run; we heard him shout S V O(S_2I).
We saw him steal the watch S V O(S_2IO_2).
We heard him tell her the story S V O(S_2 IOO_2).
We make the horse run S V O^r(S_2I).

F. Nous faisons courir le cheval S V $O^r(IS_2)$.
She made them give him bread S V $O^r(S_2IOO)$.
He made her feel happy S V $O^r(S_2IP)$.
We heard him defend himself S V $O(S_2IO(S_2))$.
I asked him not to forget to post that letter S V $O(S_2I^nO_2(IO_3))$.
I made him want to go to France S V $O^r(S_2IO_2(Ip1))$.
Their talk made me feel outside their world

$$S(S_2{}^2X) \ V \ O(S_3IP(p1(S_2{}^21)))$$.

It. L'amore fa passare il tempo, il tempo fa passare l'amore

$$S \ V \ O^r(IS_2)...$$

15. 2. Continued.

I ordered (permitted) him to fire S V O $O^r(I)$.
I ordered (permitted) the guns to be fired S V $O^r(S_2I^b)$.
G. Ich habe ihn singen hören S v $O(S_2I)$ V.
G. Ich habe das lied singen hören S v $O(O_2I)$ V.
F. J'ai entendu chanter l'actrice S V $O(IS_2)$.
F. J'ai entendu chanter la Marseillaise S V $O(IO_2)$.
F. J'entends frapper à la porte S V $O(S_2{}^0Ip1)$.
Dan. (nattergalen) Jeg har hørt den synge S V $O(S_2I)$.
Dan. (melodien) Jeg har hørt den synge S V $O(O_2I)$.
      Jeg har hørt den blive sunget S V $O(S_2I^b)$.
Dan. Han lod ham gå; G. Er liess ihn gehen S V $O^r(S_2I)$.
Dan. Han lod ham hente lægen S V $O^r(S_2IO_2)$.
G. Er liess ihn den arzt holen S V $O^r(S_2O_2I)$.
Dan. Han lod ham dræbe; G. Er liess ihn töten S V $O^r(O_2I)$.
Dan. Han lod sig barbere; G. Er liess sich rasieren

$$S \ V \ O(O_2(=S)I)$$.

F. Il fait venir le médecin S V $O^r(IS_2)$.
F. Je fais faire un habit au tailleur S V $O^r(I^*O_2pS^*)$.
F. Je fais faire un habit à mon fils S V $O^r(IO_2pO(S^21))$.
Sp. Lo haré ver á todo el mundo O^* V $O^r(I^*pS^*(21))$.
In war-time Governments find it pay to lie 3 S V $O(sIS(I_2))$.
Live and let live V & V $O^r(S^0I)$!
Let there be light V $O^r(3/s \ IS)$!

F. Voici venir le printemps $\left\{ V3 \right\}$ $O(IS)$.

    Note the absence of S in
He made believe to weep S V $O^r(S_2{}^0IO_2(S^0I))$.

15. 3. After Preposition.

We depend on you to come S W $O(S_2I)$.
I long for him to finish S W $O(S_2I)$.

15. 4. Bracketed Infinitives.

In Portuguese we have infinitives bracketed with their subject:

Êle diz sermos pobres 'he says we are poor' S V $O(\{S_2I\}P)$.

É triste combateres 'it is a pity that you fight' V P $S(\{S_2I\})$.

É uma vergonha não sabermos ler 'it is a shame that we do not know
   how to read V P $S(3^n\{S_2I\}O(I))$.

Chegou o dia de irem a côrte 'the day came for them to go to
   court' V S $p1(\{SI\}p1)$.

15. 5. Infinitive-Nexus as Subject.

L. Licet mihi esse otioso V $S(S_2 \ I \ P)$.

Middle Engl. Thow to lye by our moder is to muche shame
$$S(S_2Ip1) \ V \ P(321).$$

Sp. Perderte yo podra ser 'it may be that I lose you' $S(IOS_2)$ V.

Sp. Parece alejarse la tempestad V $S(IOS_2)$.

Old Slav. Ne dobro jesti mnogomŭ bogomŭ byti 'it is not good (for)
   many gods to be, i.e. that there are ...' 3^n P V $S(S_2(2^q1)I)$.

For her to go would be the best thing $S(pS_2I)$ V $P(21)$.

   See PhilGr 118 f.

15. 6. Infinitive-nexus as tertiary.

He proposed a picnic, he to pay the tickets and I to provide the food
$$S \ V \ O \ 3(SIO \ \& \ S_2IO_2).$$

CHAPTER 16.

Split Subject or Object.

16. 1. Passive.

There are some difficulties in the transcription of some passive
constructions.

It is easy enough, of course, to transcribe
She was seen to run (heard to cry) S V^b I,
but this simple formula does not cut deep enough, as it says nothing
of the role of the infinitive and thus does not really cover the grammatical facts. Note that in the active the object is not simply *her,*
but *her run, her cry* $O(S_2I)$. The correct notional subject of the
passive is therefore *she (to) run, she (to) cry,* though these words
are not pronounced in immediate sequence.

This analysis is even more patent when we have in the active
an O^r, as in
He made her cry S V $O^r(S_2I)$—passive
She was made to cry S V^b I.

What is made, is not *she,* but *she ... to cry.* In other words, *she*
is not the complete notional subject, though it is the "grammatical"
subject that determines the form of the verb (I am made to cry,
they are made to cry, etc.). The infinitive, too, forms part of the
subject, and this has to be symbolized.

The same consideration applies to the passive of such sentences
as "I considered this a lie", "he made her happy" (see above **14.1**).
We may, of course, write
This was considered a lie S V^b P.
She was made happy S V^b P^r,
and these symbols agree with those we should use for similar sentences
like "this seemed a lie" and "she became happy". But this analysis
does not penetrate below the surface. It is much better to treat all
these passive constructions in the same way, and the logical method
seems to be to recognize the fractional character of such "split sub-
jects" by placing the arithmetical symbol for half ($\frac{1}{2}$) before each
part, thus:
She was seen to run (heard to cry) $\frac{1}{2}$ S V^b $\frac{1}{2}$ S(I).
She was made to cry $\frac{1}{2}$ S^r V^b $\frac{1}{2}$ S^r(I).
She was made happy; The door was painted red $\frac{1}{2}$ S^r V $\frac{1}{2}$ S^r(P).
This was considered a lie $\frac{1}{2}$ S V $\frac{1}{2}$ S(P).
Dan. Varerne ønskes bragt $\frac{1}{2}$ S^r V^b $\frac{1}{2}$ S^r(P).

16. 2. Active.

Corresponding symbols are applicable to a certain class of active
constructions (MEG III 11.3 ff.), e.g.
She happened to notice it $\frac{1}{2}$ S V $\frac{1}{2}$ S(IO),—
for you could not ask "Who happened?", but "What happened?",

and the happening was her noticing it.

She failed to notice it $\frac{1}{2}$S V $\frac{1}{2}$S(IO).

She is sure to notice it $\frac{1}{2}$S V P $\frac{1}{2}$S(IO).

I place here also *seem* with an infinitive:

She seems to notice it $\frac{1}{2}$S V $\frac{1}{2}$S(IO),

for what else is the infinitive? It is not parallel to angry in "she seems angry" (S V P); but "she seems to be angry" can easily be symbolized in the way here indicated: $\frac{1}{2}$S V $\frac{1}{2}$S(IP).

Similarly F. Il semble l'approuver; G. Er scheint es zu billigen; Dan. Han synes at billige det.

16. 3. Split Object.

On account of the word-order we must use the symbol $\frac{1}{2}$ in

F. Je le croyais mort S $\frac{1}{2}$O(S$_2$) V $\frac{1}{2}$O(P).

(a. cette femme) Je l'ai entendue chanter

$$S \tfrac{1}{2}O(S^*_2) \ V \ \tfrac{1}{2}O(I^*);$$

(b. cette romance) Je l'ai entendu chanter

$$S \tfrac{1}{2}O(O^*_2) \ V \ \tfrac{1}{2}O(I^*);$$

the difference is indicated artificially in the spelling of the participle; grammarians generally call the infinitive active in (a), passive in (b). Cf. **17**.4.

F. Il m'a fait travailler S $\frac{1}{2}$O^r(S$^*_2$) V $\frac{1}{2}$O^r(I*).

F. Je lui fais faire un habit S $\frac{1}{2}$O^r(S$^*_2$) V $\frac{1}{2}$O^r(I*O$^r_2$),

if *lui* = à mon tailleur; but if *lui* = à mon fils, it is

$$S \ O \ V \ O^r(IO^r_2).$$

Du. Ik heb de kleine zien dopen S v $\frac{1}{2}$O(O$^*_2$) V $\frac{1}{2}$O(I*).

16. 4. In Relative Clauses.

The symbolization with $\frac{1}{2}$ must further be used in cases like

I met a man whom I thought dead; F. J'ai vu un homme que je
    croyais mort S V O(12($\frac{1}{2}$O$^c_2$(S$^*_2$) S V $\frac{1}{2}$O$_2$(P*))).

He spoke what we now know to be nonsense

$$S \ V \ O(\tfrac{1}{2}O_2{}^c(S^*) \ S_2 \ 3 \ V \tfrac{1}{2}O_2(I^*P)).$$

F. L'actrice que j'ai entendue chanter; Dan. Nattergalen som jeg
    har hørt synge 12($\frac{1}{2}$O^c(S) S$_2$V $\frac{1}{2}$O(I)).

F. La romance que j'ai entendu chanter; Dan. Melodien som jeg
    har hørt synge 12($\frac{1}{2}$O^c(O*) S V $\frac{1}{2}$O(I*)).

CHAPTER 17.

Infinitive.

17. 1. Subject and Predicative.

After these specimens of dependent nexus, among them also such in which there is an infinitive, we shall now proceed to the treatment of infinitives, gerunds, and nexus-substantives; but it must be remembered that these always denote a dependent nexus, even if the subject-part is not expressed (see Comments, Ch. **33**.5).

In accordance with the principle stated above (p. 5) an infinitive with *to*, G. *zu*, Du. *te*, Scand. *at*, even a F. infinitive with *à* and *de*, It. with *da*, is in most cases treated as a unit and denoted simply I instead of pI, whenever the "prefix" has lost its original prepositional force. But in Chs. **17**.7 and **18** we see examples of pI: an infinitive with a real preposition before it. Full consistency in the use of I and pI is, however, difficult to attain.

To live is to suffer; Dan. At leve er at lide S(I) V P(I).

F. Vivre, c'est souffrir S(I) s V P(I) or [S(I)] S V P(I).

To see you is a great pleasure S(IO) V P(21).

It is a great pleasure to see you s V P(21) S(IO).

F. C'est un grand plaisir de vous voir; G. Es ist ein grosses vergnügen, Sie zu sehen s V P(21) S(OI).

It.. È un gran piacere vederla V P(21) S(IO).

It is necessary to take care of her s V P S(I^{w}O).

I consider it a treat to dine here S V O(sPS$_2$(I3)).

F. À quoi bon le nier? P(p1?2) S(OI).

17. 2. Object.

He wishes to sing S V O(I).

He wants to be kind to everybody S V O(IPp1).

He is able (willing) to sing S V P(2O(I)).

He wants to see her S V O(IO$_2$).

F. Il désire la voir; G. Er wünscht sie zu sehen S V O(O$_2$I).

Ru. Dajte emu govorit' 'Give him (leave) to speak' $\left\{ \text{SV} \right\}$ O O(I) !

He had to go at once S V O(I3).

He had to say something S V O(IO$_2$).

F. J'ai à vous remercier S V O(O$_2$I).

G. Sie haben zu gehorchen; Dan. De har at lystre S V O(I).

It. Non avete da temere 3^n $\left\{ \text{SV} \right\}$ O(I).

Many questions have to be settled $S(2^q1)$ V $O(I^b)$.
He could find it in his heart to hurt her S V o pl(S^21) $O(IO_2)$.

He promised her to go S V O $O(S^0I)$.
He allowed her to go S V O $O(S_2{}^0I)$, or, more explicitly,
$$S \ V \ O \ O(S_2{}^0(=O)I).$$
The two sentences are seemingly parallel; their different import, denoted in our symbols, naturally follows from the fact that a promise refers to one's own acts, a permission to the other person's acts.

F. Dites-lui de se hâter $\begin{Bmatrix} SV \end{Bmatrix} O^* \ O(O_2{}^*I)$.
F. Il me faut aller S O V $O(IS^0 = O)$.

How is Sp. *que* to be symbolized in
Tengo que hablarte 'I have (something) to speak to you (about)'?

Possibly $\begin{Bmatrix} SV \end{Bmatrix} O(O^cIO)$.

17. 3. Infinitive as Secondary.

The life to come $12(I)$.
A book soon to appear in London $12(3Ip1)$.
The worst is still to come S V 3 $P(2=I)$.
Small comfort to those about to die 21 $pl(12(ppI))$.
Sp. Todas las academias existentes e por existir $212\&2(I)$.
You are the one to speak to the Minister S V $P(12(Ip1))$.
You are to speak to the Minister S V $P(2 = I \ pl)$.
What am I to do? $O?^*$ V S $P(2 = I^*)$.
He was the only (the first) man to protest S V $P(212(I))$.
F. Il est le premier à traiter la question S V $P(12(IO))$.
She was never one to be afraid S V 3^n $P(12(I \ P_2))$.
There are always people to believe such nonsense
$$3/s \ V \ 3 \ S(12(IO(21))).$$
F. C'est un homme à tout entreprendre S V $P(12(OI))$.
G. Er bleibt stehen S V $P(2=I)$—doubtful analysis.
Dan. Han er mand for at drikke en hel flaske S V $P(12(IO))$.
Dan. Vi savner en mand til at spille klaver S V $O(12(IO))$.
It. Una cosa da far piangere $12(IO^r(S^0I_2))$.
We found nothing to occupy us S V $O(12(IO))$.
He had no one to love him S V $O(12(IO=S))$.
A spinster with no one to love her 1^* $pl(12(IO^*))$.
She wants someone to love her S V $O(12(IO=S))$.

In these transcriptions *no one* and *someone* have been treated as units. The last sentence is really ambiguous : here *to love*, as in the preceding examples, is considered a secondary to *someone* (she wants someone who will love her)—but it may also be taken analogously to the examples given in **15**.1 (she wants (wishes) that someone may love her) ; this should be symbolized S V O(S_2IO_2(S)).

17. 4. Passive Import?

In the constructions we are next going to deal with, most grammarians will say that the infinitive, though active in form, has a passive import. This in our notation would have to be indicated by means of the oblique stroke, thus
A house to let 12($I^{a/b}$).

This conception is based on the fact that infinitives as being originally substantives are neutral with regard to "diathesis" ("turn", the distinction between active and passive)—a view which is historically (diachronically) impeccable, but which shows perhaps nothing as to the present (synchronic) feeling which it is our task to investigate and denote in our symbols.

I shall therefore in the following pages tentatively give a different analysis in which the infinitive is looked upon as active and as governing a *preceding* item as its object. This manner of viewing matters will be seen to be particularly useful in the instances treated in **17**.5, where grammarians will probably hesitate to speak of a passive meaning of the infinitive.

It is interesting to note that in a great many cases in which the other West-European languages have active infinitives, English tends to replace them by passive ones (see below **17**.6).
A house to let; F. Une maison à louer; la méthode à suivre; un
    résultat à espérer; de l'eau à boire; It. acqua da bere
$$1(O^*)2(I^*).$$
Sp. Un hecho por averiguar 'a fact to be investigated' $1(O^*)2(I^*)$
The first thing to settle; F. la première chose à décider $21(O^*)2(I^*)$.
The only thing to drink was stale beer $S(21(O^*)2(I^*))$ V $P(21)$.
This house is to let; The Cabinet is to blame $S(O^*)$ V $P(I^*)$.
F. Il est à plaindre; G. Er ist zu beklagen; Dan. Han er at beklage
$$S(O^*) \ V \ P(I^*).$$
F. Un bon résultat n'est pas à attendre; Dan. Et godt resultat er
    ikke (til) at vente; G. Ein guter erfolg ist nicht zu erwarten
$$S(O^*)(21) \ V^n \ P(I^*).$$
(Note the German development of a participle in *der zu er-*

wartende erfolg 2(Y^b)1; cf. Du. De later te behandelen vraagstuk-
ken 'the problems to be treated later on' 32(I*)1(O*).
There are many questions to settle 3/s V S(2^{q}1(O*)2(I*)).
There was no time to lose; Dan. Der var ingen tid at spilde
$$3/s \; V \; S(2^q1(O*)2(I*)).$$
There is nothing for you to do 3/s V S(1^n(O*)2(pS$_2$ I*)).

17. 5. After have, etc.

You have nothing to fear; G. Sie haben nichts zu fürchten
$$S \; V \; O(1(O_2*)2(I*)).$$
You have nothing to be afraid of; Dan. De har intet at være bange
for S V O(1(O$_2$*)2(I^w*)).
We've have got a lot to be thankful for S V O(1(O$_2$*)2(I^w*)).
He had no one to love S V O(1(O$_2$*)2(I*)).
A spinster with no one to love 1 p1(1(O*)2(I*)).
Cf. the similar, but different, example above **15.3**.
It would, of course, look simpler to write
You have nothing to fear S V O(O$_2$ I),
and correspondingly in the other cases, but it would not really express
the notional relation and would be too similar to the construction
dealt with in **15**.1—2 (Er liess ihn töten).
She wants someone to love S V O(1(O*)2(I*)).
Can you give me anything to eat?; Dan. Kan du give mig noget at
spise? v S V *O* O(1(O*)2(I*)) ?
F. Pouvez-vous me donner quelque-chose à manger?
$$v \; S \; O \; V \; O(1(O*)2(I*))?$$
She eats nothing to speak of S V O(1*2(Ip*)), or
$$S \; V \; O(1(O*)2(I^w*)).$$

17. 6. Passive Infinitive as Secondary.

This never-to-be-forgotten day 22(3^{n}I^b)1.
In a way never to be forgotten p1(12(3^{n}I^b)).
Money is not a thing to be spent rashly S V^n P(12(I^{b}3)).
This is a subject not to be mentioned before young girls
$$S \; V \; P(12(3^nI^bp1(21))).$$
The house is to be let next year S V P(I^{b}3(21)).
Such things are to be seen any day S(21) V P(I^{b}3(21)).
A good result is not to be expected S(21) V^n P(I^b).

There is nothing to be done 3/s V S(12(I^b)).
There was no time to be lost 3/s V S(2^{q}12(I^b)).
Is there nothing decent to be had? V 3/s S(122(I^b))?

Note that there is nothing corresponding to this use of the passive infinitive in any of the other West-European languages.

In some of the sentences the I has not been marked explicitly as 2.

17. 7. After Adjectives.

It is easy to deceive John; F. Il est facile de tromper Jean; Dan. Det er let at narre Jens s V P S(IO); G. Es ist leicht, Hans zu täuschen s V P S(OI).

John is easy to deceive; F. Jean est facile à tromper; Dan. Jens er let at narre; G. Hans ist leicht zu täuschen S(O*) V P(2 pI*).

It. Questa cosa è facile a sapere S(O*)(21) V P(2 pI*).

For some reason not easy to divine pO*2(3^{n}2 pI*).

F. Ceci est difficile à expliquer S(O*) V P(2 pI*)—but: Il est difficile d'expliquer ceci s V P S(IO).

This fruit is good to eat; F. Ce fruit est bon à manger; It. Questo frutto è buono a mangiare; Sp. Ese fruto es bueno de comer
S(O*)(21) V P(2 pI*).

I find this impossible to believe S V O(S$_2$(O*)P pI*).

17. 8. Analogous Cases.

This is a hard nut to crack S V P(21)(O* pI*).
He is an easy man to make fun of S V P(21)(O* pI^w*).
This is a delightful room to work in S V P(21)(1* pI p*).
This is a delightful room in which to work S V P(212(p1^c pI).
He is not an easy man to get money out of S V^n P(21)(1* pI O p*).
Such books cost a lot to print S(O*)(21) V O pI*.
I want a big room to work in S V O(21)(1* pI p*).
Sp. Pocas palabras me quedan por decir S(2^{q}1=O*) R V pI*.

In most of these (21) should perhaps stand after the starred item.

CHAPTER 18.

Infinitive Continued.

18. 1. Infinitive of Purpose, etc.

In most of the following sentences *to* before the infinitive has its original force of motion to or towards; other languages often have some other preposition before the one that corresponds to E. *to*: G. *um zu,* Dan. *for at* or *til at,* in some cases *med at,* F. *pour* with the bare infinitive. For composite prepositions we may write pp.

The infinitive with its preposition functions as a tertiary.

This led him to think deeply on the question S V O p1(I3p1).
He is inclined to welcome any stranger S V P(Yp1(IO)).
His inclination to welcome any stranger S^2Xp1(IO).
He is ready to go S V P(2pI).
He had no motive to hurt her S V O(2^q1) p1(IO).
They found an opportunity to escape S V O(XpI).
I have no time to wait; G. Ich habe keine zeit zu warten
S V O(2^q1) pI.
He came to see you S V p1(IO).
He came in order to see you S V pp1(IO).
F. Il est venu pour vous voir; G. Er kam um Sie zu sehen
S V p1(OI).
Dan. Han er kommet for at se dig; Sp. El a venido a verte
S V p1(IO).
Women are made to be loved, not to be understood S V^b pI^b,
3^n pI_2^b.
The motor car has come to stay S V pI.
We were forced to remain there S V^b p1(I3).
G. Wir waren genötigt, dort zu bleiben S V^b 3* pI*.
He will live to be ninety S V p1(IP).
He opened his eyes to find a stranger in the room S V O p1(I$O_2$3).
(She made her clothes herself, and) made them to last V O* p1(S_2*⁰I)
—different from "made them last" V O^r(S_2I).
He helped her to cook the food S V O p1($S^0_{1\&2}$ IO_2).
To understand Dickens, one must know London p1(IO) S VO_2.

18. 2. Infinitive of Reaction, etc.

I am glad to see you here S V P p1(IO3).
You were lucky to get a job S V P p1(IO).
Who am I, to quarrel with Providence? P? V S p1(I p1).
He was in a mood to cry S V P(p1pI).
Il a été deux heures à le trouver S V 3(2^q1) p1(OI).

18. 3. After too.

This is too good to be true S V P(32p1(IP₂)).
I was too tired to walk; F. J'étais trop fatigué pour marcher;
  G. Ich war zu müde um zu laufen; Dan. Jeg var for træt til
  at gå S V P(32pI).
The story is too long to amuse me S V P(32p1(IO)).
The story is too long to be impressive S V P(32p1(IP)).
The story is too long to be read at one sitting S V P(32p1(Iᵇ3)).
The story is too long to read at one sitting S* V P(32p1(IO⁰*3)).

18. 4. After Various Prepositions.

Very often an infinitive after a preposition in other languages
corresponds to an English gerund.
F. Il est parti sans vous voir; G. Er ging ohne Sie zu sehen
$$S V p1(OI).$$
Dan. Han gik uden at se Dem S V p1(IO).
F. Sans coup férir; It. Senza colpo ferire p1(OI).
F. Il est parti après avoir mangé; Dan. Han gik efter at have spist
$$S V pI.$$
It. Sto per scrivere; Sp. Voy a escribir $\left\{ SV \right\}$ pI.
G. Er ist beim anziehen S V pI.
Sp. Cuidado con hablar! 'Stop that talking!' X pI !
  Somewhat different is the construction if the infinitive is not im-
mediately dependent on the preposition, as in
G. Ich muss darauf verzichten, ihn zu überzeugen
$$S v 3(1*-p) V 1*(OI).$$
  In Portuguese in some cases the S is added:
Esta laranja é para eu comer 'this orange is for me to eat'
$$S(21) V p1(S_2I).$$
É tempo de eu partir V S p1(S₂I).
Depois de eu publicar estas linhas pp1(SIO).
  Cf. the inflected Pg. infinitive **15**.4.
  Similarly in Spanish:
Es causa bastante para tener hambre yo? 'Is that reason enough for
  me to be hungry?' S⁰ V P(12) p1(IOS)?
Murió mi tío antes del cumplir yo los trece años
$$V S(1²1) pp1(IS_2O(2ᵠ1)).$$

18. 5. Infinitive Understood:

(Can he sing? Yes,) he can S V $O^0(I)$.

(Shall you go?) I want to, but I can't S V $O^0(I)$ & S V^n $O^0(I)$.

(He wants to go) Let him! V $O(SI^0)$!

(He ran, for) I made him S V $O^r(S_2I^0)$.

(He ran when) I asked him to S V $O(S_2I^0)$.

18. 6. Infinitive in Compounds.

These cannot easily be separated from those cases in which the infinitive is treated as an adjunct and written $2(I)1$ without a hyphen; *I* here may be considered a kind of Y; cf. also

A regular sit-down supper $21(2(I3)-1)$.

Go-ahead nations $2(I3)-1$.

Stay-at-home people $2(I\ p1)-1$.

Dan. drikkepenge; sovekammer $2(I)-1$.

F. Chambre à coucher $1-2(I)$.

F. Pourboire $p-I$.

F. Savoir-vivre $I-O(I)$.

18.7. When infinitives have become substantives, especially when their meaning is concrete, they should not be symbolized I, but as ordinary primaries e.g. F. *un diner, être, devoir, pouvoir,* G. *das befinden, essen, vermögen,* It. *piacere.* The same remark applies to such English substantives as *a fight, find, look, love, wash, will,* etc., which now look as infinitives though historically in many or most cases formed independently of the infinitive.

CHAPTER 19.

Gerund.

19. 1. Ordinary.

Complimenting is lying $S(G)$ V $P(G)$.

Thinking is the most unhealthy thing (Wilde) $S(G)$ V $P(321)$.

He likes travelling S V $O(G)$.

It is no use crying s V $P(21)$ $S(G)$.

It is no use your crying s V $P(21)$ $S(S^2_2\ G)$.

It is no use you crying s V P(21) S(S$_2$G).

I remember my grandfather describing this S V O(S$_2$GO$_2$), or (S$_2$YO$_2$), if we take *describing* as a participle.

There is a chance of some wine being left 3/s V S(X pl(S$_2$G^b)).

In the beginning of the war pl(G pS).

I call that talking S V O(S$_2$P(G)).

I don't call lying in bed living S V^n O(S(G3) P(G$_2$)).

There is no denying this 3/s V S(2^{q}GO).

Is life worth living? V S P(2R(G)).

(I thank you, Jew) for teaching me that word pl(GOO(21)).

On account of there being no taxis ppl(3/sGS(2^{q}1)).

Parliament breaking up gave the officials a good excuse for doing nothing S(S$_2$G3) V O O(21 pl(GO)).

Sophia's having seen them did not surprise us S(S$_2$^{2}GO) V^n O$_2$.

Sophia's being seen by them ... S(S$_2$^{2} G^b pS$_3$) ...

19. 2. Passive Meaning?

The garden wants weeding S(O*) V O(G*), or S V O(G$^{a/b}$).

This will be the making of you S V P(GpO).

This will be your undoing S V P(O^{2}G).

He was dissatisfied with his own bringing up S V P(Y^{b}pl(O^2*2G*)).

19. 3. With Adjectives and Adverbs.

On account of his deliberate buying up of stocks ppl(S^{2}2(3)GpO).

On account of deliberately buying up stocks ppl(3 G O).

The best cure is the rapid carrying out of social reforms

$$S(2X) \ V \ P(2(3) \ G* \ pl(O*{=}2X)).$$

The best cure is carrying out social reforms rapidly

$$S(2X) \ V \ P(G \ O(2X)3).$$

Forgive my plain speaking $\left\{ SV \right\} O(S^2 2(3)G)$!

Forgive my speaking plainly $\left\{ SV \right\} O(S^2 \ G3)$!

Men must endure their going hence, even as their coming hither

$$S \ V \ O(S^2G3 \ \& \ S^2G_23).$$

19. 4. Gerund in Compounds.

Walking-stick 2(G)-1.

Sleep-walking 2-G.

Walking-excursion 2(G)-X.

Bed-sitting-room 2(2 &⁰ G)-1.

Dancing-master (stress on first part) 2(G)-Y.

(But ¹*dancing* ¹ *master* with stress on both parts 2(Y)1.)

Short story writing pays well S(2(O = 21)-G) V 3.

Glasgow Iron Ship Building Yard 2-1(2(2(O(2-1))-G)-1) : *Glasgow* defines all the rest; *Iron* defines *Ship; Iron Ship* is the object of *Building.*

A house-warming (= house-warming party) 2(2(O)-G)-1⁰.

All the examples given in this chapter are English, because the English Gerund presents some peculiarities not found in the other languages dealt with in this book. The so-called gerunds of It., Sp. and Pg. (ending in *-ndo*) are rather to be considered active participles and should be symbolized Y. The only exception is the use after the preposition Sp. *en,* Pg. *em,* F. *en:* en diciendo esto, cf. F. en disant cela p1(GO). Here the G may even have a S:

Sp. en cenando yo 'when I have dined' p1(GS).

Pg. em êle chegando 'when he arrives' p1(SG).

19. 4. Concrete.

When an English gerund has acquired a concrete signification, it should be symbolized like any ordinary substantive and not written down as G, e.g. *drawing* (= G. zeichnung, F. dessin), *building* (= G. gebäude, F. édifice), *knitting, shavings.*

CHAPTER 20.

Nexus-Substantives.

20. 1. Various Examples.

Activity produces happiness S(X) V Oʳ(X₂).

His suggestion; her kindness S²X.

His education S²Xᵇ = O²Xᵃ.

Her reception of the guests S²X pO.

(In this and the following examples pO and pS should properly be marked 2(pO) and 2(pS) corresponding to the notation in **3**.4.)

The control of mind X pO.

The control of mind over matter X pS pO.

The control of matter by mind X pO pS.

The discovery of America; F. La découverte de l'Amérique X pO.

The discoveries of Columbus; F. Les découvertes de Colomb X pS.
The advance of science X pS.
The advancement of science X pO.
L. Expugnatio oppidi; G. Die eroberung der stadt XO^2.
L. Amor, patris, according to circumstances XS^2 or XO^2.
L. Memoria nostri tia X $2(O^2)2(S^2)$.
It. L'amore della madre X pS.
It. L'amore per la madre X pO.
They witnessed massacres of Christians by Chinese S V O(XpO_2pS_2).
Then occurred his expulsion from power by the Tories
$$3 \ V \ S(O^2Xp1pS_2).$$
(Lady Byron's dealings with Byron in the long period of) her court-
  ship by and of him $1^2X \ pS^0$ & pO.
The prohibition of night work by women and children
$$X \ pO(2\text{-}X_2 \ p1(S \ \& \ S_2)).$$
This needs explanation S V O$(X^{a/b})$ or S(O^*) V O(X^*).
J'en vois la nécessité S $2(S)^*$ V O(X^*).

20. 2. With Adjectives and Adverbs.

Some important discoveries 2^q2X.
No new examination of the room had taken place S(2^q2XpO) V O_2.
His hard work stopped S$(S_2^22(3)X)$ V; cf. he worked hard S V 3.
Her extreme youth surprised us S$(S_2^22(3)X)$ V O; cf. she was
  extremely young S V P(32).
A careful examination; perfect simplicity; a positive impossibility
$$2(3)X.$$
He was in favour of virtual free trade S W O$(2(3)2X)$.
F. L'amour excessif de soi X2(3)pO$(=S)$.
Dan. I forholdsvis ro; med nogenlunde sikkerhed p1$(2(3)X)$.
Our stay here; Dan. Vort ophold her; G. Unser aufenthalt hier
$$S^2X2(3).$$

20. 3. Nexus-Substantives in Compounds.

Sunrise; earthquake; G. sonnenaufgang; Dan. solopgang 2(S)-X.
Sun-worship; childbirth; G. sonnenanbetung; Dan. soldyrkelse
$$2(O)\text{-}X.$$
Washstand 2(X)-1.
Lip-service 2-X.
A mutual admiration society 2(2X)-1.

Italian war-preparations 21(2(O)-X).
Civil service 2-X, or 2mX.
She lost self-control S V O(2(O*=S)-X*).
Self-sacrifice; G. selbstopfer 2(O=S)-X.

20. 4. Nexus-Substantive in Apposition.

A nexus-substantive may stand in apposition to an adjective:
Her face was very pale, a greyish pallor S V P(32) [2X].
He had been too proud to ask—the terrible pride of the benefactor
S V P(32*pI) [2X* pY].
These examples were given in PhilGr. 138, where it was also mentioned that what is termed by grammarians "the cognate object" may really be looked upon as a nexus-substantive (generally with an adjective) standing in apposition to a verb, thus Mowgli laughed a little short ugly laugh S V [222X].
Kitty laughed—a laugh musical, but malicious S V [X2 & 2].
See the treatment of the whole subject in MEG III 12.3.
Cf. also: His hair was brown—a deep brown colour
S(1²1) V P [2(2-2)1].

20. 5. Concrete.

It should be noted that nexus-substantives are often used in a concrete signification:
The *Government* acted swiftly and effectively.
She was the *beauty* of the village.
His *possessions* were enormous.
Such cases must be treated as ordinary primaries without indicating the origin of the substantives.

CHAPTER 21.

Agent-Substantives and Participles.
(These are here classed together and denoted Y).

21. 1. Agent Substantives.
The discoverer of America Y pO or Y2(pO)
His supporters O²Y.

We are your debtors S V P(O^2Y).

He is a hard worker; a loose liver; an early riser; a prospective buyer S V P(2(3)Y).

A close student of geometry; a regular reader of the *Times*
2(3)Y pO.

A young student of geometry 2Y pO.

A believer in the Trinity Y pO.

A great theatre-goer 2(3)1(2-Y), cf. *great friends* above **3**.6.

A looker-on Y^w.

G. Alexander war der besieger der ganzen welt S V P(YO^2(21)).

21. 2. Participles, etc.

An admired employer; G. Ein bewunderter lehrer; Dan. En beundret lærer 2(Y^b)Y^a.

An admiring employee; G. Ein bewundernder lehrling; Dan. En beundrende lærling 2(Y^a)Y^b.

A well-constructed plot 2(3Y^b)1.

We separate the known from the unknown S V O(Y^b) pY^{nb}.

A German speaking Italian 12(YO).

A German-speaking Italian 2(OY)1.

A thought-inspiring book; Dan. En tankevækkende bog; G. Eine welterschütternde begebenheit 2(OY)1.

A kind-looking girl 2(PY)1—but: A good-looking girl 2(3Y)1.

A learned man; a drunken woman 2($Y^{b/a}$)1.

A well-spoken (well-behaved) lad 2(3$Y^{b/a}$)1.

The young girl waiting on us 212(Y^wO).

There is an answer waiting 3/s V S P($Y^{a/b}$), or 3/s V S(O*) P(Y*).

F. Paris et les villes environnantes 1 & 1(12(Y))

F. Les villes environnant Paris 12(YO).

F. Une rue passante 12($Y^{a/b}$).

F. Un homme très connu 12(3Y^b).

F. La lettre confiée à lui par Jean 12(Y^bpOpS^a).

G. Ein reizendes gemälde 2(Y)1.

G. Die deinem vater gehörenden sachen 2(R($1^2$1)Y)1.

G. Die höher gebildeten 2(3)Y.

G. Die besser bezahlten beamten 2(32(Y))1.

He had the book bound (his fortune told); Dan. Han fik bogen indbundet S V O^r(S_2P(Y^b)).

He had the horse shot under him; Dan. Han fik hesten skudt bort under sig S V O(S_2P(Y^bpS)).

The difference between the two is that in the former the result is the effect of the subject's acting—and only in such instances should the symbol O^r be employed—; in the latter sentence the shooting of the horse happened without the subject's will.

In these Danish sentences *fik* is unstressed; but if we stress *fik* in *han fik bogen indbundet,* the meaning is different ('he received the book bound', i.e. in a bound condition) : S V O [Y^b].

It is difficult to analyze

G. Es wurde [N.B. sg.] karten gespielt s V S(OY) or S v O V^b.

21. 3. Apposition.

Discovering us, he shouted [YO] S V.

He listened amazed S* V [Y*].

He returned, utterly exhausted S* V [3Y*].

I found him in the ditch, utterly exhausted S V O* 3(p1) [3Y*].

She was left standing alone in the street S V^b [Y(2)P3(p1)].

While travelling in Russia, he was arrested [3^{c}Y(2)3(p1)] S V^b.

G. Er kam gelaufen S V [Y$^{b/a}$].

21. 4. Adjectives, etc.

G. Er ist der französischen sprache mächtig (kundig) ; Dan. Han er det franske sprog mægtig S V P(O(21)Y).

G. Er blieb ihm die antwort schuldig; Dan. Han blev ham svaret skyldig S V P(*O* O Y).

G. Ich bin mir keines unrechts bewusst; Dan. Jeg er mig intet ondt bevidst S V P(*O* O(2^{q}1) Y).

Oblivious of everything Y pO.

L. Homo avidus laudis 12(YO^2).

F. Un homme avide de sang 12(YpO).

In the following examples a verbal form which is not a participle plays, as it were, the role of one.

A tumble-down hut 2(Y3)1.

Mock-turtle-soup 2(YO)1.

Mock-heroic poems 2(YO(P))1.

A would-be wit 2(YI*)1(P*).

This symbolization is specially difficult, because *wit* besides being the primary to which *would-be* is an adjunct, is also predicative of *be,* one part of the composite Y; cf. above **3**.7.

One might also think of writing *would-be* as Y^w.

21. 5. Y in Compounds.

Innkeeper; shoemaker; house-owner; G. schuhmacher; Dan. sko-mager $2(O)$-Y.

Rope-dancer; sleep-walker; eye-witness; G. seiltänzer; Dan. line-danser; søvngænger 2-Y.

Loud-speaker; forerunner; F. avant-coureur; G. vorläufer; Dan. højttaler; forløber $2(3)$-Y.

Wireless operator $2(O)$-Y or 2^m-Y.

Godsend $2(S)$-Y.

A sunburnt face; a tailor-made dress; a God-forsaken country
$$2(2(S^a)\text{-}Y^b)1.$$

London-made goods; hand-made shoes; Dan. håndgjorte sko
$$2(2\text{-}Y^b)1.$$

Ready-made clothes; a free-born Roman; Dan. færdigsyet tøj
$$2(P\text{-}Y^b)1.$$

A God-fearing man $2(O\text{-}Y)1$.

Non-smoker; Dan. ikke-ryger; G. nicht-raucher $2(3)^n$-Y.

Civil servant $2+Y$ or 2^mY.

F. Cerf-volant $1+2(Y)$.

A self-conscious man; G. ein selbstbewusster mann; Dan. en selv-bevidst mand $2(O{=}S\text{-}Y)1$; but the adjectives do not mean the same thing.

Gk. patroktónos 'parricide' O-Y^a; patróktonos 'killed by his father' S-Y^b (thus Vendryes, Le langage 91; but the actual occurrence of the latter seems doubtful).

In the following instances the base of the verb is used:

Pickpocket; breakwater; F. porte-manteau; perce-neige; It. passa-tempo, spazza-cammino; Sp. templa-plumas; G. wippsterz
$$Y\text{-}2(O)\ ;\ \text{cf. } \mathbf{39}.2.$$

A run-away slave $2(Y3)\text{-}1$ or $2(Y3)1$, if *run* is taken as the participle.

A non-stop train $2(Y^n)\text{-}1$.

A go-between Y-$2(3)$.

Cp. F. réveil-matin Y-$2(3)$.

CHAPTER 22

Clauses as Primaries.

22. 1. Content-Clauses.

That he is ill is indubitable $S(3^c\ S_2\ V\ P)\ V\ P_2$.

G. Dass er krank ist, ist sicher $S(3^c\ S_2\ P\ V)\ V\ P_2$.

I believe that he is ill S V O(3^c S$_2$ V P).

G. Ich denke, dass er krank ist S V O(3^c S$_2$ P V).

I believe he is ill; G. Ich denke, er ist krank S V O(S$_2$ V P).

It is certain that he is ill; F. Il est certain qu'il est malade

s V P S(3^c S$_2$ V P$_2$).

Too bad, that he should be ill P(32) S(3^c S$_2$ V P$_2$).

I think it probable that he is ill S V O(s P S$_2$(3^c S$_3$ V P$_2$)).

I know nothing except that he is ill S V O pl(3^c S$_2$ V P).

You overlook the fact that he is ill S V O [3^c S$_2$ V P].

Her idea that he will die is absurd S(1^21 [3^c S V]) V P.

I am not sure he is ill S V^n P p^{0}l(S$_2$ V P$_2$) ; cf., however, **36**.3.

F. Pas vrai? elle est charmante; Dan. Ikke sandt, hun er sød?

P(3^n2 ?) S (S$_2$ V P$_2$).

What do you suppose had happened? S$_2$*? v S V O(V*).

What do you suppose he said? O$_2$*? v S V O(S$_2$V*).

In these two one cannot consider *do you suppose* as a mere parenthetical insertion (which should be symbolized by [ ]), but the final words are really objects of *suppose;* otherwise we should in the latter sentence have had *did he say.* Cf. Dan. "Hvad tror du der var sket?" and "Hvad tror du han sagde?" The stars show that *what* is the subject, resp. the object of the final V. Thus also:

How old did you say she was? P*(3?2) v S V O(S$_2$V*).

22. 2. Continued.

Dan. Det ærgrer mig at jeg ikke kan komme; Du. Het spijt me dat ik niet komen kan s V O S($3^cS_2 3^nV$).

G. Mich freut es, dass du singen wirst O V s S(3^cS_2V).

I take it that you will pay S V o O(3^c S$_2$ V).

It never struck him that Bolshies are human beings

s 3^n V O S(3^c S$_2$ V P).

He never gave it a thought that Bolshies are human beings

S 3^n V *o* O O(3^c S$_2$ V P).

Dan. Jeg håber ikke det vil regne S V 3^n* O(S$_2$ V*).

No wonder that he is angry P(2^q1) S (3^c S$_2$ V P$_2$).

F. Cela tient à ce qu'ils sont mariées S V pl(3^c S$_2$ V P).

F. Il faut que tu viennes S V O(3^c S$_2$ V).

22. 3. Dependent Questions (Interrogative Clauses).

I wonder is he ill? S V O(V S$_2$ P ?).

I don't know if (whether) he is ill S v^n V O(3^c S$_2$ V P ?).

G. Ich weiss nicht, ob er krank ist S V 3^n O(3^c S_2 P V ?).

G. Dann wird (es) sich zeigen, ob er kommen wird

$$3 \text{ v (s) O V S}(3^c \text{ } S_2 \text{ V ?}).$$

F. Je me demande si c'est vrai S *O* V O(3^c S_2 V P ?).

When he leaves he always tells us when he will be back

$$3(3^c \text{ S V) S } 3 \text{ V } O \text{ O}(3^c? \text{ S V } 3).$$

G. Wenn er geht, sagt er immer, wann er zurück kommen wird

$$3(3^c \text{ S V) V S } 3 \text{ O}(3^c? \text{ S } 3 \text{ V}).$$

It does not interest me whether he is ill or not

$$\text{s } V^n \text{ O S}(3^c \text{ } S_2 \text{ V P \& } 3^n?).$$

It does not interest me who is ill s V^n O S(S_2? V P).

How he did it is another problem S(3^c? S_2 V O) V P(21).

F. Comment il l'a fait, c'est une autre question; G. Wie er das

getan hat, das ist eine andere frage [3^c? S_2 O V] S V P(21).

I should like to know how and why he did it

$$\text{S V O}(I \text{ } O_2(3^c? \text{ \& } 3^c_2? \text{ } S_2 \text{ V O}).$$

He will give an account of why he did it S V O p1(3^c? S V O).

I do not know the reason why he did it S V^n O [3^c? S V O].

This is why he was afraid S V P(3^c? S_2 V P).

I have no idea of what you charge me with

$$\text{S V O}(2^q1 \text{ p1}(1^*? \text{ } S_2 \text{ V Op*}).$$

He had no idea how this should be done S V O(2^q1) [3^c? S_2 V^b].

He was puzzled by the question, who had killed the man

$$\text{S } V^b \text{ p1 } [S_2? \text{ V O}].$$

22. 4. Infinitive in Dependent Questions.

He knows how to play S V O(3? I).

I don't know what to think S v^n V O(O_2? I).

F. Je ne sais pas que penser S 3^* V 3^{n*} O(O_2? I).

Ru. Ja ne znal čto delat' 'I did not know what to do'

$$\text{S } 3^n \text{ V O}(O_2? \text{ I}).$$

22. 5. Relative Clauses as Primaries.

Who steals my purse steals trash S(S^c V O) V O_2.

Whoever says that is a liar S(S^c V O) V P.

Lat. Qui boni sunt amantur S(S^c P V) V^b.

F. Qui dort dîne S(S^c V) V.

G. Wer etwas wünscht, der sage es S(S^c O V) s V O! or

$$[S^c \text{ O V] S V O!}$$

What you say is quite true S(O^c S$_2$ V) V P(32).
What I want is money P(O^{c}SV) V S$_2$, or S(O^{c}S$_2$V) V P.
He took what he wanted S V O(O^{c}SV).
He took what money I had S V O(O$_2$(2^{c}1) S$_2$ V).
What money I have is at your disposal
$$S(O(2^c1)\ S_2\ V)\ V\ P(p1(1^2X)).$$
He was angry with whoever crossed his path S V P p1(S$_2$^{c}VO(1^{2}1)).
Whom the gods love die young S*(O^{c}S$_2$V) V [2*].
You may dance with whom you like S V p1(O^{c}SV).
F. Il raconte l'histoire à qui veut l'entendre S V O p*O*(S^{c}vOV).
Things are not what they seem S V^n P(P^{c}SV).
This is what publishers would like us to read S V P(O*S$_2$VO(S$_3$I*)).
This is where you are mistaken S V P(3^{c}S$_2$V).
He ran away from where he had been lying S V 3 p1(3^{c}SV).

CHAPTER 23.

Clauses as Secondaries.

23. 1. With Pronouns.

The man who killed Jaurès was not punished; F. L'homme qui a
  tué Jaurès n'a pas été puni S(12(S^c V O)) V^{bn}.
The man whom he killed was Jaurès; F. L'homme qu'il a tué était J.
$$S(12(O^c\ S_2\ V))\ V\ P.$$
F. Je sens mes jambes qui tremblent encore S V O(1^{2}12(S^c V 3)).
F. Une chambre dont la porte était fermée 12(S(2^{c}1) V P(Y^b)).
These poems which you admire were written by Heine; F. Ces poè-
  mes que vous admirez ont été écrits par Heine; G. Diese ge-
  dichte, die Sie bewundern, sind von Heine geschrieben
$$S(212(O^c\ S_2\ V))\ V^b\ pS^a.$$
Heine, whose poems you admire, was a German Jew; G. Heine,
  dessen gedichte Sie bewundern, war ein deutscher jude
$$S(12(O(1^{2c}1)\ S_2\ V))\ V\ P(21).$$
F. Heine, dont vous admirez les poèmes, était un juif allemand
$$S(12(1^{2c*}\ S_2\ V\ O^*))\ V\ P(12).$$
F. Ce qu'il me faut c'est de l'argent S(12(O^{c}S$_2$*O*V) s V P.
I dislike the way in which he treats children S V O(12(p1^c S$_2$ V O)).
F. Le couteau dont je me sers 12(O$_2$^{c}SO(S)V).

23. 2. Continued.

The man was mad who married her S* V P 2*(Sᶜ V O).
They should take who have the power S* V 2*(Sᶜ V O).
People are coming whom we have not asked S* V 2*(Oᶜ S₂ Vⁿ).
F. Jean était là qui nous regardait S* V 3 2*(Sᶜ O V).
F. Tout est bien qui finit bien S* V P 2*(Sᶜ V 3).
F. (banquiers) J'en connais qui sont honnêtes S O* V 2*(Sᶜ V P).
Un livre dont j'ai lu le commencement 12(2ᶜ* S V O*).
All that glisters is not gold S(1*2(3ᶜ V)) V 3ⁿ* P.
G. Es ist nicht alles gold was glänzt s V 2*(3ⁿ2 q) P S*(SᶜV).
    On these sentences see Negation, p. 87.
I have nothing with which to cut S V O(12(p1ᶜ I)).
Sp. Nada he que replicar O* {SV} 2*(OᶜI).

23. 3. Relative Adverbs.

You mentioned the town where I was born S V O(12(3ᶜS₂Vᵇ)).
In the year when I was born p1(12(3ᶜSVᵇ)).
G. Dies ist das haus wo er getötet wurde S V P(12(3ᶜS₂Vᵇ)).
F. C'est ici la maison où il a été tué S V 3 P(12(3ᶜS₂Vᵇ)).
G. Frankfurt ist die stadt, woher er kam S V P(12(3ᶜS₂V)).
F. J'admire la manière dont il joue S V O(12(3ᶜS₂V)).
F. Son silence est la seule chose dont je suis surpris
                              S(S₂²X) V P(212(3ᶜS₃VP)).
G. Das messer, womit er schneiden wollte, war stumpf
                              S(12(1ᶜ-pS₂V)) V P.
(F. Une chambre très comme il faut 132(3ᶜSV).)

23. 4. That.

This is the key that was lost yesterday S V P(12(3ᶜ/Sᶜ Vᵇ 3)).
This is the key that you lost yesterday S V P(3ᶜ/Oᶜ S₂ V 3)).
I've found the key that you spoke of S V O(12(3ᶜ/1ᶜ*S₂ V p*)).
All is well that ends well S* V P 2*(3ᶜ/Sᶜ V 3).
He is not the bright fellow that he used to be
                              S Vⁿ P(212(3ᶜ/Pᶜ S V).
The carrier was in high spirits, good fellow that he was
                        S* V P(p1) [*P(21) 3ᶜ/Pᶜ S V].
Mrs. Harrison, Miss Brown that was 11 [P(11) 3ᶜ/Sᶜ V].
Fool that you are!; F. Fou que tu es! 12(3ᶜ/Pᶜ S V).

I never saw him, that I remember S 3^n V O $3(3^c$ S V).

He came on the same day that this happened S V p1$(212(3^c$ S_2 V)).

By the time that you are dressed, breakfast will be ready

p1$(12(3^c$ S V P$))S_2$ V P.

Now that you are ready, we may have breakfast $3(3^c$ S V P) S_2 V O.

F. Un jour qu'il était malade, il m'appela

$3(12(3^c$ S V P)) S O V.

On relative *that* and *as* see Comments **40**.1.

23. 5. As, Than, But.

Such people as knew him intimately admired him

S$(212(3^c/S^c$ V O 3)) V O.

You must put up with such answers as I can give

S W O$(212(3^c/O^c$ S_2 V)).

These are not such opinions as men fight for

S V^n P$(212(3^c/1^{c*}$ S_2 V p^*)).

I know the family secrets, young as I am S* V O(2-1) [*P 3^c S V].

As usually happens, the criminal got away $3(3^c/S^c$ 3 V) S V 3.

He is a brave man, as are all his friends

S V P(21) $3(3^c/P^c$ V $S_2(2^q1^21)$).

He offers more than could be expected S V O$(13(3^c/S^c$ V^b)).

He offers more than we could expect S V O$(13(3^c/O^c$ S_2 V)).

There are no ladies there but keep a dog

3/s V S(2^q1^*) 3 2*$(3^c/S^c$ V O).

23. 6. Relative Contact Clauses.

I've got the book you want; Dan. Jeg har den bog du søger

S V O$(O_2^*$ 2$(S_2$ V*)).

(An easier, but not so exact notation would be S V O$(12(O^{c0}$ S_2 V)).

Correspondingly in the following specimens.)

The seed ye sow another reaps O(O* 2(S V*)) S_2 V.

The book you want is here; Dan. Den bog du søger ligger her

S(O* 2$(S_2$ V*)) V 3.

This is the book you want S V P(O* 2$(S_2$ V*)).

You are not the first I've said no to; Dan. Du er ikke den første

jeg har sagt nej til S V^n P(1* 2$(S_2$ V O p^*)).

I don't know the man Mary is talking to S V^n O(1* 2$(S_2$ V p^*)), or

S V^n O$(O_2^*$ 2$(S_2$ W*)).

He is not the giant he was; Dan. Han er ikke den kæmpe han var
$$S \ V^n \ P(P^* \ 2(S \ V^*)).$$
There are few would believe that 3/s V S(S* 2(V* O)).

23. 7. Concatenated Clauses.

People whom she knew he despised 12(O^{c*} S V O(S$_2$ V*))— or
$$12(O^c \ [S \ V] \ S_2 \ V).$$
Cakes which whosoever tasted would desire to taste again
$$12(O^{c*} \ S(S^cV^*) \ V \ O(I^*3)).$$
Dan. Yndigheder som den må være blind der ej kan se hos eder
$$12(O^{c*} \ S^{**} \ V \ P \ 2^{**}(S^c \ 3^n \ V^* \ p1)).$$
Can you mention anyone we know who is really happy?
$$v \ S \ V \ O(O^*2(S \ V^*)2(S^cV3P)?$$
Is there anything you want which I can get for you?
$$V \ 3/s \ S(O^*2(S_2V^*)2(O^cS_3Vp1)?$$
A thing which I don't know where to place
$$12(O^{c*} \ S \ V^nO_2(3?^cI^*)).$$
I argued against everything he believed had happened
$$S \ W \ O(S_2^*S_3VO_2(V^*)).$$
We feed children who(m) we think are hungry
$$S \ V \ O(12(O^c/S^c_2 \ S \ V \ V_2 \ P)):$$
On the analysis see MEG III 10.7 and PhilGr 349 ff; *are hungry*
should be marked as O of *think*; possibly
$$S \ V \ O(\tfrac{1}{2}O_2{}^c \ S \ V\tfrac{1}{2}O_2(VP)).$$
F. Ce mot que je crois qui est d'Alfieri 212(3^c S V S$_2$^{c} V p1)—see
Sandfeld, Syntaxe II § 126; analysis really impossible.

CHAPTER 24.

Clauses as Tertiaries.

24. 1. Simple Conjunctions.

He will not turn up if he is ill; F. Il ne viendra pas s'il est malade
$$S \ V^n \ 3(3^c \ S \ V \ P).$$
He did not call because he was ill; F. Il n'est pas venu parce qu'il
était malade S V^n 3(3^c S V P).
When she sees John she laughs; F. Quand elle voit Jean elle rit
$$3(3^c \ S \ V \ O) \ S \ V.$$

He ran away because he was afraid; Dan. Han stak av fordi han
var bange S V 3 3(3^c S V P).
He did not stay in because he was ill (but for some other reason)
$$S v 3^{n*} V 3 3^*(3^c S V P).$$
We burst out laughing when we saw him
$$S V 3 Y 3(3^c S V O).$$
Dan. Vi brast i latter da vi så ham S V pl 3(3^c S V O).
G. Wir brachen in ein gelächter aus, als wir ihn sahen
$$S V^* pl 3^* 3(3^c S O V).$$
F. Nous avons éclaté de rire quand nous l'avons vu
$$S V pI 3(3^c S O V).$$
G. Wir lachten, als wir ihn laufen sahen S V 3(3^c S O(S$_2$I) V).
Whenever they meet they quarrel 3(3^c S V) S V.
Once his resolution was taken, he never hesitated
$$3(3^c S(S_2{}^2X) V^b) S_2 3^n V.$$
Suppose the war breaks out, what will you do?
$$3(VO(S_2V 3))O_2? v S V, or 3(3^cS_2V3), etc.$$

24. 2. Composite Conjunctions.

I have no objection as long as you are content
$$S V O(2^qX) 3(3^{cc} S_2 V P).$$
We can leave as soon as you are ready; Dan. Vi kan køre, så snart
(som) du er færdig S V 3(3^{cc} S$_2$ V P).
G. Wir können abreisen, so bald du fertig bist
$$S V 3(3^{cc} S_2 P V).$$
He hid the watch for fear it should be stolen
$$S V O 3(3^{cc} S_2 V^b).$$
As soon as she sees John she laughs; F. Aussitôt qu'elle voit Jean
elle rit 3(3^{cc} S V O) S V.
She laughed as if she were mad; F. Elle riait comme si elle était
folle S V 3(3^{cc} S V P).

24. 3. So that, etc.

Things move so fast that we cannot follow S V 43 3(3^c S$_2$ V^n).
Things move fast, so that we cannot follow S V 3 3(3^{cc} S$_2$ V^n).

Come here that I may introduce you{ SV } 3 3(3^c S V O)!
He came forward in order that I might introduce him
$$S V 3 3(3^{cc} S_2 V O).$$

G. Kommen Sie hierher, damit ich Sie vorstellen kann

$$V \ S \ 3 \ 3(3^c \ S_2 \ O \ V) \ !$$

F. J'ouvre la porte afin que tu puisses entrer S V O $3(3^{cc} \ S_2 \ V)$.

24. 4. Prepositions and Conjunctions.

We wait till he comes; Dan. Vi venter til han kommer; G. Wir
    warten, bis er kommt S V p1 $(S_2 \ V)$.

F. Nous attendons jusqu'à ce qu'il arrive S V pp1 $(3^c \ S_2 \ V)$.

I shall see you before you leave; Dan. Jeg skal se dig for du rejser

$$S \ V \ O \ p1(S_2 \ V).$$

F. Je vous verrai avant que vous partiez S O V p1 $(3^c \ S_2 \ V)$.

After he had gone, we went to bed p1(S V) S_2 V p1, or $3(3^c$ S V),

etc.

G. Nachdem er gegangen war, gingen wir zu bett

$$3(3^c \ S \ V) \ V \ S_2 \ p1.$$

Dan. Efterat han var gået, gik vi i seng $3(3^c$ S V) V S p1, or

$$p1(3^c \ S, \ etc.$$

F. Dès qu'il est parti nous nous sommes couchés

$$p1(3^c \ S \ V) \ S_2 \ O(S_2) \ V.$$

In a different way when the preposition enters into composition
with an adverb (cf. above under Infinitive **18**.4) :

G. Sie können sich darauf verlassen, dass er bezahlen wird

$$S \ v \ O(S) \ 3(1\text{*-}p) \ V \ 1\text{*}(3^c \ S_2 \ V).$$

G. Es kommt darauf an, ob er bezahlen wird

$$S \ V\text{*} \ 3(1\text{**-}p) \ 3\text{*} \ 1\text{**}(3^c \ S_2 \ V).$$

24. 5. Various Combinations.

I'll answer next time I see you S V $3(212(3^{co}$ S V O)) or

$$\ldots 3((21)^c \ S \ VO).$$

I know the way she speaks S V O $(12(3^{co} \ S_2 \ V))$.

You may go anywhere you like S V $3(32(3^{co}$ S V))—or

$$S \ V \ 3(3^c \ S \ V) ;$$

    cf. You must go directly you see him S V $3(3^c$ S V O).

Every time she sees John she laughs 3 $(212(3^{co}$ S V O)) S V, or

$$3((21)^c \ S\ldots$$

F. Chaque fois qu'elle voit Jean elle rit $3(212(3^c$ S V O)) S V.

24. 6. Word-Order.

Had he been alive, we should have seen him 3(v S V P) S_2 V O.

G. Kommt er, dann töte ich ihn 3(V S) 3 V S_2 O.

Dan. Kommer han, så slår jeg ham ihjel 3(V S) 3 V S₂ O 3.

F. Je l'épouserais, fût-elle pauvre S O V 3(V S₂ P).

He speaks as he did yesterday S V 3(3ᶜ S V 3).

Tom is as big as John; F. Louis est aussi grand que Jean;
   G. Max ist ebenso gross wie Hans S V P(32 3ᶜ S₂).

I hate him just as much as he me S V O 3(543 3ᶜ S₂ O₂).

24. 7. Comparison.

I love him better than he me S V O 3 3ᶜ S₂ Vᵒ O₂.

I love him better than John S V O 3 3ᶜ S₂ Vᵒ Oᵒ, or, according to
   circumstances, ... Sᵒ Vᵒ O₂.

He offers more than we expected S V O(1 3ᶜ S₂ V Oᵒ₂).

He offers more than could be expected S V O(1 3ᶜ Sᵒ₂ Vᵇ).

The more we know, the more harm we can do each other
$$3(3ᶜ \text{ O S V}) \text{ O}(32^q1) \text{ S V } O(\text{S}_x).$$

The older he grows, the more he drinks 3(3ᶜ P S V)ꞏO(31) S V.

The better I know him, the more I love him
$$3(4ᶜ3 \text{ S V O}) \text{ 43 S V O}.$$

F. Plus je connais les hommes, plus j'admire les animaux
$$3(3ᶜ \text{ S V O}) \text{ 3 S V O}_2.$$

Sp. Cuanto mas trabaja, menos posee 'the more he works, the less
   he possesses' 3(43 Sᵒ V) O Sᵒ V.

F. Plus on boit de bière Carlsberg, plus on aide la science
$$3(2^{qc*} \text{ S V pO}*(12)) \text{ 3 S V O}_2.$$

24. 8. Indifference.

I hate him, whatever you say S V O 3(Oᶜ S₂ V).

I hate him, however much you love him S V O 3(4ᶜ3 S₂ V O).

I shall go, whether you approve or not; F. J'irai, que vous approu-
   viez ou non S V 3(3ᶜ S₂ V & 3ⁿ).

G. Du musst bleiben, ob er reist oder nicht S V 3(3ᶜ S₂ V & 3ⁿ).

I shall go, no matter what you say S V 3(P(2^q1) S₂(Oᶜ S₃ V)).

Dan. Jeg rejser, lige meget hvad du siger S V 3(P(31) S₂(Oᶜ S₃ V)).

F. Je la suivrai, n'importe où elle va S O V 3(3ⁿ V S₂(3ᶜS₃V)).

24. 9. Abbreviated Clause.

She always knits her brows when thinking hard
$$\text{S}* \text{ 3 V O 3}(3ᶜ \text{ Y}* \text{ 3}).$$

He may have heard us, but if so he did not show it
$$S \ V \ O \ \& \ 3(3^c3) \ S \ V^n \ O_2.$$
G. Er kommt vielleicht, aber wenn nicht, dann ist es gleichgültig
$$S \ V \ 3 \ \& \ 3(3^c3^n) \ 3 \ V \ S_2 \ P.$$
F. Bien que socialiste, il vote pour le gouvernement
$$3(3^c \ P) \ S \ V \ p1.$$

CHAPTER 25.

Parenthetic Clauses.

25. 1. Ordinary Parenthetic Remarks.

This, I think, (or, This, it seems,) is madness $S \ [S_2 \ V] \ V \ P.$
It was fortunate, he thought, that the rain had stopped
$$s \ V \ P \ [S_2 \ V] \ S(3^c \ S_3 \ V).$$
G. Er ist, scheint es, ganz unschuldig; Dan. Han er, synes det, helt
    uskyldig; F. Il est, semble-t-il, absolument innocent
$$S \ V \ [V \ S_2] \ P(32).$$
Sp. El socorro que esperanban habia de venir $12(S^c \ [S^o \ V] \ V \ O(I))$.
If, as you think, the war is coming $3(3^c \ [3^c \ S \ V] \ S_2 \ V)$.

25. 2. Referring to a Whole Sentence.

A relative clause may stand in apposition to a whole sentence or idea. In this case we indicate by means of the position of the sign § if it refers to what precedes or to what follows.

I have come to-day, which you will excuse $S \ V \ 3[\S \ O^c \ S_2 \ V]$.
I go there whenever I have time, which isn't often
$$S \ V \ 3 \ 3(3^cSVO) \ [\S \ S^cV^nP(3)].$$
He said nothing, and, what is worse, laughed at us
$$S \ V \ O \ \& \ [S^cVP \ \S] \ W \ O.$$
If, which very seldom happens, there are two geniuses in a family
$$3^c \ [S^c43V \ \S] \ 3/s \ V \ S(2^q1) \ p1.$$
F. Il est aimé de tous, ce qui s'explique par son charme
$$S \ V^b \ p1(S^a) \ [\S \ 12(S_2^cOVp1(1^21))].$$

25. 3. Symbolization of it is.

The following instances must be kept distinct.

(a) *It* is anaphoric, i.e. refers back to something previously mentioned or evident from the situation:

(My hat. Where is it?) It is here, on the table $S \ V \ 3 \ p1.$

(What colour is her new dress?) It is blue S V P.
(I met him in London. When was that?) It was last Christmas
S V 3(21).
(b) Unspecified *it*:
It is cold to-day; it is dark in here S V P 3; cf. it rains, etc.
It is too early to go to bed S V P(32) p1(I p1)).
(c) Anticipative or preparatory *it* as a "dummy subject".
It is dreadful to suffer s V P S(I).
It was good that you could come s V P S(3c S₂ V).

This *it* is specially useful by making it possible to stow away
for a moment a long string of words which would make the sentence
top-heavy if it were placed where a subject or object is usually
placed.

25. 4. Cleft Sentences.

(d) A fourth class of sentences beginning with *it is* will form the
chief contents of this chapter. They were dealt with in MEG III
4.6, where I said[1] that in "it is the wife that decides" and "it was
the Colonel I was looking for" what we mean is really "the wife
is the deciding person" and "the Colonel was the man I was looking
for"; the relative clause thus might be said to belong to *it* rather
than to the predicative following after *it is*.

This, I said, explains the possibility of having a *that*-clause or a
contact-clause (i.e. one without any relative word) after a word
which is in itself so definite that it cannot be further restricted: It
was the battle of Waterloo that decided the fate of Europe, etc. In
other words the clause is felt to be, and is treated like, a restrictive
clause, though it does not logically restrict the word with which it
is connected.

According to this view we should symbolize:
It is the wife who decides S* V P 2*(S₂c V).

I said also that Chaucer's "it am I That loveth so hote Emelye
the brighte" has become "it is I (me)"; but what about the person
of the verb in the relative clause? Chaucer has the third person,
which agrees with the logical analysis given above[2], but most people

---

[1] As already briefly in Danish, Sprogets logik (1913), p. 59.
[2] Curme, Syntax 187, quotes my remarks and speaks of *am* as "incorrect"
in "It's not I that am marvellous" instead of the correct *is*.—Tobler,
Verm. beiträge 1.160 calls "c'est moi qui suis le maître" illogical, and
finds "ce n'est pas moi qui suis le maître" noch seltsamer.

will take the relative clause to define the pronoun and therefore write "It is you that (or, who) are guilty", and even in the negative: "It is not I who am guilty". This is also the French rule: "C'est vous qui l'avez fait, ce n'est pas moi qui suis le coupable".

A similar view is found in Kr. Sandfeld, *Syntaxe du Français Contemporain* (1936), p. 119 ff.: *Ce fut le pasteur qui fut étonné* is looked upon as a "transposition" of the "primitive" construction *Qui fut étonné, ce fut le pasteur.* The transposition "a eu pour con-séquence que la nature de la proposition relative indépendante a été méconnue et qu'elle a été confondue avec les propositions rela-tives adjointes". This is shown in the form of the verb, which should be invariably in the third person, instead of which we say *C'est moi qui l'ai fait, c'est toi qui l'as fait,* etc. "La langue populaire, toute-fois, a gardé la forme primitive de la proposition relative", e.g. *C'est moi qui le paiera.*

25. 5. Criticism.

The necessity of finding the best way of symbolizing such sentences has given me occasion to re-consider the whole question. I shall leave out of account the question of the origin of such constructions: Sandfeld may, or may not, be right in what he says about "primitive". What interests me is how they are felt now, and how they are accordingly to be analyzed and symbolized. And here it is certainly worth noting the striking conformity found between French and English, and, let me add, Danish. The relative clause is always joined very closely with its antecedent—with what accord-ing to the view expressed above is only seemingly its antecedent: no pause is tolerated, the intonation shows close coherence, in Eng-lish and Danish contact-clauses (without any relative word) are admitted, and in English *that* is used preferably to *who* or *which*. The ordinary French and English punctuation does not tolerate a com-ma before the relative clause. The almost universal agreement with regard to person and number of the verb in the relative clause with the immediate antecedent points in the same direction, i.e. against the transposition theory.

Further the transposition theory breaks down where there is no pronoun corresponding to *it,* as in It. "Quando è un santo che parla, è il Signore che lo fa parlare" (Manzoni). "Siete voi che volete inebriarmi" (d'Annunzio).

Nor can this theory easily account for those cases in which it is not a substantive or a pronoun, but an adverb or a similar word that follows after *it is*. *It was here that he died, C'est ici qu'il mourut:* this could not be said to be = *That he died was here, Qu'il mourut est ici*—and it is far removed from *Where he died was here, Là où il mourut c'est ici.* Is *that* (*que*) here a relative word, or is it the same "conjunction" that we have in "I think that he died here, Je crois qu'il mourut ici"? Danish here has *at*, which corresponds to *that, que* in the sentences just mentioned: *Det var her at han døde*—or without any connecting word: *Det var her han døde.* (In vulgar Danish *at* is used even in *Det var Jens at jeg saa* 'it was John that I saw'.) And what can be made of F. *est-ce-que* (*est-ce-que Pierre viendra*), which evidently is a case in point—is the clause following *que* relative?

Note also that in the question "Who was it that shouted?", "Qui est-ce qui a crié?", the natural stress is laid on *was, est,* and not on the following pronoun, *it, ce,* though otherwise the word preceding a restrictive relative clause is stressed[1]; a stressed *it* (instead of *that*) is quite impossible in English before a relative pronoun. The constrast is evident with "Who was he that shouted?", "Qui est celui qui a crié?", Dan. "Hvem var han som råbte?" with stress on *he, celui, han* —i.e. on the words restricted by the relative clause. All this goes to show that the relative clause is not to be termed restrictive with regard to *it, ce, det.*

Why do people use this paraphrase with *it is?*

In MEG III I simply mention these clauses as restrictive clauses introduced by *it is*, but say nothing about the purpose of *it is*. Sandfeld says that the construction "sert d'ordinaire à identifier le sujet et l'attribut: *c'est mon frère qui a dit cela le premier* nous apprend qui est la personne en question et équivaut à: *celui qui a dit cela le premier, c'est mon frère* ou bien: *mon frère est celui qui a dit cela le premier*".

It is often said that the insertion of *it is* serves to give emphasis to the word thus singled out. But this is not quite correct. Emphasis is better given by stress and (or) intonation, and these phonetic means generally accompany the construction we are dealing with, but they might have been—and often are—used with effect even without employment of the *it is*-construction. Emphasis (and stress) is even frequently laid on another word than the one singled out by being made the predicative of *it is,* thus the adverb in "It is always

[1] In Dan. *Hvem var det som råbte?* we may stress either *var* or *det*.

the wife that decides" or "It is never the wife that decides". I should, therefore, rather say that the construction with *it is* serves as a demonstrative gesture to point at one particular part of the sentence to which the attention of the hearer is to be drawn especially. In some, though not in all cases, this construction may be considered one of the means by which the disadvantages of having a comparatively rigid grammatical word-order (SVO) can be obviated[1]. This explains why it is that similar constructions are not found, or are not used extensively, in languages in which the word-order is considerably less rigid than in English, French, or the Scandinavian languages, thus German, Spanish and Slavic.

25. 6. Symbolization.

I now propose to take this *it is* (*is it*) together with the connective word (if any such is found) as a kind of extraposition, symbolized [ ], and to treat the rest of the sentence as if there had been no intercalation;—thus *wife* in the first example is not marked as P; s and v are written as "lesser subject and verb":

It is the wife that decides [sv] S [3^c] V.

It is the wife who decides; F. C'est la femme qui décide [sv] S [s^c] V.

F. C'est le ton qui fait la musique [sv] S [s^c] V O.

F. C'est Jean que nous avons vu [sv] O [o^c] S V.

It was John we saw; Dan. Det var Jens vi så [sv] O S V.

It was the colonel I was looking for; Dan. Det var oversten jeg ventede på [sv] O S W.

It is I who pay; F. C'est moi qui paie; Dan. Det er mig der betaler [sv] S [s^c] V.

It is I have been stupid [sv] S V P.

It was John he gave the money to [sv] 1* S V O p*.

Who was it saw her S? [vs] V O.

Who is it that cries? S? [vs3^c] V.

How much money was it he stole? O(32^q?1) [vs] S V.

What is it you're talking of? O? [vs] S W.

It is only the milk that is bad [sv] 3 S [3^c] V P.

It is a poor heart that never rejoices [sv] S(21) [3^c] 3^n V.

Similar sentences are collected MEG III 4.6$_2$ with the explana-

---

[1] I have dealt elsewhere with related compromises between the order SV and the interrogative order VS (does he come / Pierre vient-il / est-ce que Pierre vient) and between the wish to have a negative soon and to have it after the verb (he doesn't come).

tion: The meaning obviously is "the heart that never rejoices is poor"—but this shows that transposition gives no natural clue to the construction.

F. Qui est-ce qui crie? S? [vss^c] V.
F. Qui est-ce que tu as vu? O? [vso^c] S V.
F. Qu'est-ce qui est arrivé? S? [vss^c] V.
F. Qu'est-ce que tu as vu? O? [vso^c] S V.

These four French forms fall a little out of focus: French has really developed a composite inflected interrogative pronoun: S animate [kjɛski], O animate [kjɛskə], S inanimate [kɛski], O inanimate [kɛskə].

We are now in a position to transcribe two interesting sentences which in print look the same though in actual speech they differ by their intonation:

It is the country that suits her best—either
(a) S V P(12(3^c/S^c V O 3))—or
(b) [sv] S [3^c] V O 3.

The example is taken from Maria Schubiger, "The Role of Intonation" (St. Gallen, 1935, p. 17); but her explanation is insufficient: "With the first intonation [stress both on *country*, on *suits*, on *her*, and on *best*] the sentence is complex, with the second [stress only on *country*] the construction is a means to bring into relief the psychological predicate". In (a) the contrast is between two countries, one of them mentioned previously (*it* anaphoric) in (b) between country and town life; this is indicated in the Danish translation, in (a) *det land*, in (b) *landet*.

The advantage of our notation is seen with double relative clauses (MEG III 4.6$_6$), e.g.

It is only people who know him well that praise him
[sv] 3 S(12(S^c V O 3)) [3^c] V O.
F. C'est la poule qui chante qui a fait l'œuf
[sv] S(12(S^c V)) [s^c] V O.

25. 7. With Tertiaries.

It is here he must come; Dan. Det er her slaget skal stå [sv] 3 S V.
It is here that he must come; Dan. Det er her at slaget skal stå
[sv] 3 [3^c] S V.
It was yesterday he died; Dan. Det var igår han døde [sv] 3 S V.
It was yesterday that he died; F. C'est hier qu'il est mort
[sv] 3 [3^c] S V.

When was it he died?; Dan. Når var det han døde? 3? [vs] S V.

When was it that he died?; Dan. Når var det at han døde?; F. Quand est-ce qu'il est mort? 3? [vs3^c] S V.

It was in Paris that he met Mary; F. C'est à Paris qu'il a rencontré Marie [sv] p1 [3^c] S V O.

F. C'est à Jeanne qu'il a écrit la lettre [sv] p1 [3^c] S V O.

But there is some difficulty with our symbolization of sentences like:

It was Joan to whom he wrote the letter; F. C'est Jeanne à qui il a écrit la lettre.—It is perhaps best to transcribe [sv] 1p [3^c] S V O —though I confess that this is a little awkward.

Sp. De un rey es de quien hablamos p1 [v p1^c] $\left\{SV\right\}$; in French the corresponding phrases (C'est à vous à qui je parle) were formerly usual; now they are considered incorrect.

It was because he was ill that he did not come; F. C'est parce qu'il était malade qu'il n'est pas venu; Dan. Det var fordi han var syg at han ikke kom [sv] 3(3^{c}SVP) [3^c] SV^n.

F. Est-ce que Pierre viendra? [vs3^c] S V ?

F. Quand est-ce que Pierre viendra? 3? [vs3^c] S V.

But *Est-ce (Est-il) vrai que Pierre viendra?* is different:

$$V \ s \ P \ S(3^c \ S_2 \ V) \ ?$$

25. 8. German and Scandinavian.

As already remarked, the cleaving of sentences by means of *it is* and corresponding formulas is not very frequent in German, yet we find, e.g.,

Es waren tapfere männer die uns angegriffen hatten

[s v] S(21) [s^c] O V.

In

Es ist blosser neid, was aus ihm spricht [s v] S(21) [s^c] p1 V, we note the neuter *was* corresponding to *es,* not to *neid.* Comparatively frequent are word-orders like the following, and it is worth noting that though the relative pronoun corresponds to the person, not to *es,* this does not influence the person of the verb in the clause:

Sie waren es, der anfing; Du warst es, der anfing S [v s s^c] V.

Ich bin es, der es getan hat S [v s s^c] O V.[1]

---

[1] From my reading I have noted Schnitzler, Prof. Bernhardi 188 Wenn sich hier einer zu entfernen hat, so bin das selbstverständlich ich / Bischoff, Am. Dietrich 264 Bin dann ich das, die hier so allein herumwandert?

Cf. on the other hand Sp. Yo soy el que lo digo S [v p s^c] O V and even con quien hablaba es contigo (Valdés, Sinf. past. 15).

In the examples so far given we found always the simple verb *is* (*was*) ; but in the Scandinavian languages we have also the verb *bliver, blir* which expresses the "ingressive aspect", e.g.
Dan. Det blir Jens der betaler [sv] S [s^c] V.
Det blev Jens der betalte [sv] S [s^c] V.
The meaning is approximately expressed in English and French by the translations : 'Is is John that will (have to) pay ; It came to be John that paid ; C'est Jean qui paiera ; Ce fut Jean qui dut payer'.

25. 9. Speaker's Aside.

Denoted by $<\ >$.
Talking of golf, have you met Nelson lately? $<$Y p1$>$ v S V O 3? ⸳
Oddly enough, I met him yesterday $<$34$>$ S V O 3.
Strange to say, I met him yesterday $<$2 pI$>$ S V O 3.
He is a regular magician S V P($<$2$>$ 1).
He fairly screamed S $<$3$>$ V.
It amounted to practically nothing S V p$<$3$>$1.
He kind of smiled S $<$1p$>$V.
He smiled like S V $<$3$>$.
He fell rather than climbed into bed S V $<$33^c V$>$ p1.

A full account of such asides as Linguistic Self-Criticism will appear in Tract 48 of the Society for Pure English ; cf. also Sproglig selvkritik (Det ottende nord. filologmøde 1935, p. 33 ff.).

CHAPTER 26.

Amorphous Sentences.

26. 1. Introduction.

Many sentences cannot be analyzed as containing a nexus. They consist of only one member, though this may contain more than one word. While the sentences of complete predicational nexuses are (often, at any rate) intellectual and formed so as to satisfy the strict requirements of logicians, amorphous sentences are more suitable for the emotional side of human nature. When anyone wants to give vent to a strong feeling he does not stop to consider the logical analysis of his ideas, but language furnishes him with various adequate means of bringing the state of his mind to the consciousness of his hearer or hearers.

Such amorphous sentences range from sounds which are not otherwise used in ordinary speech, such as the click (suction-stop) of compassion, annoyance or impatience, conventionally, but imperfectly, written *tut* or *tck*, through single ordinary speech sounds like [ʃ·] to enjoin silence (conventionally spelt *hush*), or sound-combinations like *hm!* or *ha ha!* and conventional "interjections" like *alas! hullo!* or *hurra!* to single words or word-combinations capable of being used also in full nexus-sentences.

Fully unanalyzable sentences are here denoted **Z**:

ʃ· and clicks, etc. **Z**!

Yes! **Z**!

Goodbye! **Z**!

26. 2. Half-analyzable Sentences.

Not a few sentences which some grammarians would probably reckon among amorphous sentences have been placed here and there among our examples of analyzable phenomena, e.g. "Splendid!" (9.6) and "Silence!" (13.1). When a substantive stands alone it is often impossible to decide whether it should be regarded as the subject or an object of an imaginary verb: those who are fond of explaining grammatical facts by means of ellipses are often at liberty to choose either explanation. When the street-criers shout "Strawberries!" is this to be taken as subject or object? As Madvig somewhere remarks we know accidentally that in ancient Rome such cries were in the accusative and thus felt as object, for the cry "Cauneas!" ('Figs!') was taken as a warning not to go, as it was pronounced like "Caue ne eas!" G. "Guten morgen!" in the accusative may similarly be taken as the object (of something like "Ich wünsche Ihnen"), but there is nothing to show whether E. "Good morning!", Dan. „God dag!" is S or O.

Therefore I write 1 instead of a possible S or O in cases like the following (cp. also instances in **13**.1.):

O, these women! Z 1(21)!

What about a drink? 1? p1.

Hence his financial difficulties 3 $1(1^2 21)$ (this rather like S).

F. Après nous le déluge! p1 1!

G. Viel geschrei, wenig wolle 2^q1 2^q1.

Thanks! | John! | Heavens! | An aeroplane! 1!

Thanks awfully! 13!

Similarly X without specifying if S or what else in

F. Défense de fumer X pO(I).

When we say "Good, isn't it?" we use first a kind of amorphous sentence, and then improve it by adding a verbal question P, V^n S?

In telegraphese and in newspaper headlines half-analyzable sentences abound, e.g.

Taken wrong train; returning to-morrow V O(21) V 3.

Young girl shot by mistake S(21) Y^b p1, or O(21) V p1.

But it should be remembered that sentences of this kind occur chiefly or exclusively in writing. See the full treatment in H. Straumann, Newspaper Headlines (London 1935).

26. 3. Answer.

In answers unanalyzable or half-analyzable sentences abound; but generally they may be symbolized in the same way as if they were members of sentences corresponding to the question:

(Who said it?)—John. S.

(Whom did you see?)—Mary. O.

(Is he rich or poor?)—Poor. P.

(When did it happen?)—Yesterday. 3.

(Are you coming?)—Of course. p1.

(How is it done?)—Thus. 3 (with a gesture).

There are some words which are used exclusively in answers, namely *Yes* and *No*. These fall outside our ordinary symbols, and are, as remarked above, denoted by the letter Z.

26. 4. Retort.

In retorts, too, various more or less unanalyzable sentence-forms are frequent, e.g.

(You unmitigated idiot!)—Idiot yourself! P S.

(I want my revenge)—You and your revenge! 1 & $1^2$1.

F. Toi et ton cinéma! 1 & $1^2$1.

Dan. (Han har ingen apparater)—Du med dine apparater!

$$1 \ p1(1^2 1).$$

26. 5. Amorphous Combinations.

In proverbial sayings we often find two members of which the first amorphously expresses a condition and the second what happens when the condition is fulfilled: No cure, no pay = 'if there is no cure there will be no pay'. We may tentatively and crudely symbolize them as follows, 3 implying the condition as a tertiary in the sentence as a whole:

No cure, no pay $3(2^q1)$ 2^q1.

Least said, soonest mended $3(SY^b)$ 3 $P(Y^b)$.

First come, first served $3(3Y)$ 3 $P(Y^b)$, or $P(3Y^b)$.

Like master, like man $3(21)$ 21.

One man one vote $3(2^q1)$ 2^q1.

G. Klein geld, kleine arbeit $3(21)$ 21.

F. Point d'argent, point de suisse $3(2^qp1)$ 2^qp1.

26. 6. Clauses.

We have amorphous clauses in:

(Will he come?) I hope so S V O(3).

I hope not S V $O(3^n)$—cf. **24**.9.

F. J'espère que oui S V $O(3^cZ)$; thus also *que non*.

26. 7. Deprecation.

He a miser! F. Lui avare! Dan. Han gerrig! G. Der ein geizhals! S P^{no}! (the meaning is: "How can you say that he is a miser?" By an unintentional coincidence our symbols for negation ^{n} and not-expressed ^{o} together look as the answer to the question).

G. Judenhetzer anständige leute! S $P(21)^{no}$!

She talk to him! Dan. Han gifte sig med hende! S $Ip1^{no}$!

F. Toi faire ça! It. Io far questo! S V O^{no}!

Lat. Mene incepto desistere victam? S* 3? O I $[Y^{b*}]^{no}$!

Sp. Olvidarla yo? I O S^{no}! = I forget her! S I O^{no}!

CHAPTER 27.

Complicated specimens.

Finally let us analyze a few rather complicated specimens.

27. 1. From Samuel Johnson.

The   proverbial   oracles   of   our   parsimonious   ancestors   have
  S(2   1   p1(1^2 2   1))

informed us, that the fatal waste of our fortune is by small expenses,
V   O O(3^c S$_2$ (2 X pO(1^2 1)) V pl 2   1)
by the profusion of sums too little singly to alarm our caution,
[p   X   p O(1 3   2 3(3   I   O(1^2 X)))
and which we never suffer ourselves to consider together.
& 2(O^{c*} S$_3$ 3^n V O(S$_3$ I*   3))))].

27. 2. Brother Juniper.

Brother Juniper, forgetting everything except the brother's wishes,
S(1   1   2(Y   O   pl(1^2 1))
hastened to the kitchen, where he seized a knife, and thence directed
V   p   1   2(3^c S V   O & 3   V
his steps straightway to the wood where he knew the pigs to be
O(S^2 1)   3   p   1   2(3^c S V O(S$_2$ I)
feeding.

Compare with this the pictorial analysis in Isabel Fry, A Key
to Language, London 1925, p. 64:

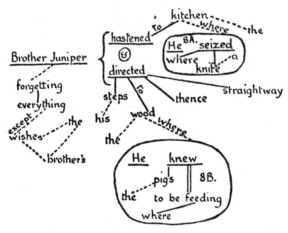

Her diagram on p. 83 is even more forbidding, though done with
extreme care.

27. 3. From a German Newspaper (quoted by Hammerich).

Ein in allen einzelheiten auf tendenziösen darstellungen
2(4(pl(2   1))   3(p   1(2   1))
aufgebauter und infolgedessen ganz unverlässiger bericht über die
2   &   4(pl)   3   2   1(X p

dividendenpolitik der stahl- und eisenfabriken der Saar.
　1(2-X)　　　1²(2(2　　&　　2)-1)　　1²)).

27. 4. From Cicero.

Credo ego vos, iudices, mirari, quid sit, quod, cum tot summi
$\left\{SV\right\}$ [S] O(S_2 [1]　　　I O(S_3? V　3^c　3(3^c 2^q　2

oratores hominesque nobilissimi sedeant, ego potissimum surrexerim,
　Y　&　1　　　　2　　　V)　[S*]　　3　　　$\left\{S{*}V\right\}$

qui neque aetate neque ingenio neque auctoritate sim cum iis, qui
2*(S^c &^{n}　3　&^{n}　3　&^{n}　3 $\left\{SV\right\}$ P(p1(12($S_3{}^c$

sedeant, comparandus.
　V)　　　Y)))).

PART II
COMMENTS

CHAPTER 28.

General.

28. 1. Previous Attempts.

So far as I know, this is the first complete attempt at a systematic symbolization of the chief elements of sentence-structure, though we meet here and there with partial symbolizations, as when the letters SVO and SOV are used to indicate various types of word-order. A. Stöhr's "Algebra der grammatik" (Leipzig 1898) is of a totally different order and seems rather fantastic; a few specimens may be given:

$a *{}^{1}_{g}$ = ein männliches a.

$a *{}^{2}_{g}$ = ein weibliches a.

${}^{1}_{t}$ = irgend etwas in der vergangenheit.

${}^{2}_{t}$ = irgend etwas in der gegenwart.

${}^{3}_{t}$ = irgend etwas in der zukunft.

${}^{4}_{t}$ = irgend etwas zu allen zeiten.

${}^{2}_{e}$ = modus dubitativus.

${}^{3}_{e}$ = modus optativus.

${}^{4}_{e}$ = modus imperativus.

${}^{1}_{n}$ = irgend etwas notwendiges.

${}^{2}_{n}$ = irgend etwas unmögliches.

${}^{3}_{n}$ = irgend etwas mögliches.

${}^{5}_{i} \left(a *{}^{1}_{h}\right)$ = das (a hier).

${}^{15}_{i} \left(a *{}^{1}_{h}\right)$ = dem (a hier).

Further comments are certainly superfluous.

Maurice Bologne's "Analyse grammaticale à l'aide de Signes conventionnels" (Liège, 1935) gives fanciful signs (triangles, squares, arrows, etc.) for various grammatical categories.

Mention must also be made of E. Sapir's system of denoting analysis (cutting-up) of words into their constituents (Language, 1921, ch. II). Roots or stems are denoted by capitals, grammatical elements by small letters. Elements that cannot stand alone are placed in round brackets. Examples :

fire-engine A + B.

sings, singer A + (b).

L. hortus (A) + (b).

sing A + (0) : it belongs to the A + (b) type in which (b) has vanished. L. cor (A) — with the minus-sign to denote that something is lost of the full stem as shown in *cordis,* etc.

There may of course enter more elements than these, the formula for an American Indian word analyzed by Sapir is $(F)+(E)+C+d+A+B+(g)+(h)+(i)+(0)$.

It will easily be seen that all this is totally different from the system here attempted : it is pure morphology.

28. 2. Brøndal.

Much more important than any of the otners is Viggo Brøndal's elaborate system, see "Morfologi og Syntax" (København 1932) and the previous book "Ordklasserne, Partes Orationis" (ib. 1928, avec un résumé en français). Brøndal builds up a remarkable logical system applicable to all languages and having as its basis four fundamental categories—and only those—, which he denotes and symbolizes as follows :

1. Relation = relator (r),
2. Substance = relatum (R),
3. Quality = descriptor (d),
4. Quantity or basis (frame) = descriptum (D).

By means of these, singly or combined in various ways, Brøndal constructs an elaborate system of word-classes, viz.

A. Abstract :

Prepositions (r) : *de* ;

Proper names (R) : *Platon* ;

Adverbs (d) : *bien* ;

Numerals (D) : *cinq.*

B. Concrete:
Nouns (Rd) : *parisien*;
Verbs (rd) : *être*;
Pronouns (RD) : *ce*;
Conjunctions (rD) : *que*;
Possessives (rR) : *mon, mien*;
Reflexives (dD) : *se, soi*.

C. Complex:
Derived Verbs (Drd) : *rougir, rougissant*;
Derived nouns (DRd) : *parleur, aimable*;
Derived pronouns (numerals) (rDR) : *premier, moi*;
Verbal nouns (rdR) : *pensée, sagesse*.

D. Undifferentiated:
Interjections (rRdD) : *Oh! Oui!*

Subclasses depend on one or another element being particularly stressed, thus Nouns (Rd) may be either substantives (**Rd**), or adjectives (**Rd**).

One of Brøndal's chief tenets is the autonomy of each of the two great divisions, morphology and syntax: in morphology (word-classes, cases, etc.) it is strictly prohibited to apply syntactic categories, and vice versa. One is therefore perhaps a little surprised in coming from the morphological to the syntactic part to find exactly the same symbols, only, it is true, with the addition of a colon, so that some of the main categories are denoted in the following way:

Subject D :d,
Object r :R,
Predicate r :d.

Here, too, we may have subdivisions, according as the stress is laid on one or the other element, thus in Fr. "moi je travaille" *moi* is **D** :d and *je* D :**d**.

The whole is highly ingenious (just as the Linnean system of botany is ingenious), and Brøndal's books are full of shrewd critical remarks. But I hope I may be forgiven for thinking that his system with its shifting about of the four symbols is too much of an intellectual *tour-de-force* to fit the linguistical facts: language, i.e. the human mind, cannot be pressed into so strict a frame. Some of the views, e.g. about proper names and reflexives, appear to be extremely disputable, even paradoxical. It is not easy always to see the purport of his four categories, more particularly when they appear combined, and I must confess that when after an absence from his writings of a month or so I ask myself, what is meant by Dr or rD, the exact purport has slipped completely out of my mind,—though that, of course, may be due to a deficiency in my individual mental equipment.[1]

Brøndal's method is avowedly (see "Morf. og Synt.", p. 58) to set up first of all the theoretical possibilities of combinations of his *D, r,* etc., and afterwards to make an attempt at finding them again (genfinde dem) in actual sentences: he succeeds, but not always without a visible effort. My own method has been diametrically opposite: I have everywhere started from sentences as occurring in actual living speech and have then tried to find out what they stand for and how they are to be understood and analyzed, making extensive use of traditional terms—while recognizing all the imperfections and deficiencies of existing terminology—and trying to construct on this basis a set of concise and easily memorable formulas.

My aim is a much more modest one than Brøndal's, as I do not pretend to create a logical system for human language in general. In the first instance I wanted to understand and systematize the principal phenomena of the sentence structure of that one language which I have studied with special care, English, and thus to provide a means of distinguishing and describing all the various types found there. As, however, in analyzing English, I had to consider constantly the question, what is specially characteristic of that language, and

---

[1] Brøndal on more than one occasion freely criticizes my own views, but that has not hindered him from dedicating his "Morfologi og Syntax" to me. In the same way my own opposition to some of his opinions does not detract from my admiration for his learning and brilliancy.

  If we take Brøndal's terms descriptor and descriptum at their face value and then try to apply them to the combination "that grey-bearded journalist Jones", we may say: *grey* describes *beard* and is a descriptor (d), *beard* in relation to *grey* is descriptum (D), but it also describes the man, or rather, *grey-bearded* is descriptor (d) to the descriptum (D) *journalist,* but this latter word, or the whole complex, is descriptor to *Jones* (D). But this proper name which here is D, in other connexions may be called descriptor (d), for if you answer the question "Whom did you meet?" by saying "Jones", this to those who know him contains a whole description. But in Brøndal's system a proper name is relatum (R) and has nothing to do with D or d. Thus we see that common-sense use of Brøndal's terms leads us nowhere, at any rate not to Brøndal's system.

what may be termed universal, applicable to all human languages, or at all events to many languages (for the variety in language structure is so enormous that no single scholar dares to speak of all), I was gradually led to include examples from a dozen other languages, both where they agreed with and where they differed from English. In one respect I am, no doubt, more ambitious than Brøndal, for I have gone into much more detail than he has, and have dealt with many more concrete problems than are touched on in his books.

28. 3. My Own.

In constructing a system based chiefly on the use of capital letters I was encountered by difficulties arising from the fact that so many of the usual grammatical terms begin with the same letter. Thus, the following letters might stand each for any of the ensuing terms:

A: Active Adjective Adjunct Adnex Adverb Apposition Attribute Auxiliary.

C: Compound Conjunction Connective.

I: Imperative Indefinite Indirect Infinitive Ing Interrogative.

N: Negation Nexus (Nexus-substantive) Noun.

O: Object Nought (cipher).

P: Participle Particle Passive Past Perfect Person Predicate Predicative Preposition Preterit Primary Pronoun.

R: Recipient Reciprocal Reflexive Regimen Relative.

S: Secondary Subject Subjunct Substantive.

Under these circumstances a selection had to be made, and after a good deal of experimenting I arrived at the symbols enumerated in Chapter 2 and illustrated in the rest of Part I. It must be admitted that X, Y, and Z are chosen arbitrarily, though X may remind one of the medial x in Nexus.

28. 4. Meaning of the Small Letters.

Why have the small symbols, s, o, *o*, and v, been devised?

To avoid misunderstanding it may not be superfluous to say expressly that they are not meant for some inferior kinds of subjects, objects, etc., exemplified by such short pronominal forms as F. *je*, *me* (as contrasted with *moi*), etc. *Je* and *le* in *Je le raconte* are symbolized S and O and are for our purposes on exactly the same footing as *Jean raconte l'histoire.* Therefore we write S, not s, for the subject in *It rains, Il pleut, Es regnet,* etc.

The chief reason for these symbols is practical convenience. The small s and o are extremely handy for what I have elsewhere called preparatory *it.* This may be considered the real subject and object, respectively, in cases like "It is a great pleasure to see you" and "We have it in our power to do great harm", while the infinitive is put in extraposition (or, if you like, in apposition) at the end of the sentence. This may be written:

S*V P(21) [*IO]—and

S V O* p1(S²1) [*IO$_2$(21)].[1]

It is, however, more convenient, and, by the way, more in accordance with the natural feeling of the unsophisticated mind, to look upon *it* as a mere preliminary or introductory word, a foreboding of the real subject, "a dummy subject", and thus to write:

s V P(21) S(IO) and

S V o p1(S²1) O(IO$_2$(21)).

Similarly when *it* prepares a whole clause as subject or object. The same remark holds good for the corresponding pronouns in other languages, *il, ce, es, det,* etc. Examples are found in Chapters **22-24.**

It is also more convenient to transcribe familiar French sentences like "Henri viendra-t-il?" as S V s? rather than putting *Henri* in extraposition: [1*] V S*?

With the small v the case is similar, but not exactly the same. It is best, for the sake of convenience, to take forms like *will drink, would drink, shall drink, should drink, has drunk, had drunk, is drinking, has been drinking,* even *can drink, may drink,* etc., as wholes to be simply symbolized V. A more explicit but inconvenient way of symbolizing is the following:

He will drink whisky; he should drink whisky, he can drink whisky

      S V O(IO$_2$)—with the infinitive as (part of) the object—

He is drinking whisky S V P(YO).

He has drunk whisky S V O(Y$^{b/a}$ O$_2$).

He has been drinking whisky S V O(YP(Y$_2$O$_2$)).

So, instead, we write simply S V O for all of these.

---

[1] Cf. He is a humbug, that man Cranby, whom you seem to admire so much
S* V P [21*2 etc.].

Now, this would be very plain sailing everywhere but for the rules which oblige speakers to separate these elements of a composite V in certain well-defined cases, when either the S or a tertiary is intercalated after the first element, and it is this that makes the small v so valuable an instrument:

Will (shall, would, should, can, may, must ...) he drink whisky?
                                                          v S V O?

Has (had) he drunk (been drinking) whisky? v S V O?

Will he be drinking whisky? v S V O?

He will (would, etc.) always (on all occasions, under no circumstances, etc.) drink whisky S v 3 V O.

Note that V after a small v stands sometimes for an infinitive, sometimes for a participle.

It was a different chain of reasoning that led to the adoption of the small p. This should properly be a capital like the other big letters, but the place of P happened to be occupied for another purpose, where it could not be easily replaced, viz. for Predicative; hence p, which thus does not at all stand in the same relation to P as o does to O or v to V. Compare the necessity of appropriating the small index ^{b} instead of ^{p} for passive.

We shall now deal at greater length than was possible in Part I with some of the most difficult problems involved in our scheme.

28. 5. What not symbolized.

In order properly to understand the purpose of the system it may be well here at once to state what is *not* symbolized in it. Cf. **41**.2.

It has no reference to the *signification* of the words or sentences indicated: whether S is a king or a peasant, a place or a feeling, whether 2 is big or small or heavenly or abominable, whether V is love or hate or see or omit, etc., all such things have no influence on the symbols.[1]

The only exception is the index for negation, ^{n}. This exception is justified by the influence negation has in many languages on sentence structure, see, for instance, English *don't, won't,* and especially the Finnish verbal forms:

---

[1] Therefore such an idiomatic expression as F. *Je lui en veux* 'I bear him a grudge' with "unspecified *en*" must be symbolized in the same way as (de l'argent) *Je lui en donne* 'I give him some' with "specified *en*": S *O* O V.

En tuo I do not bring,
Et tuo thou dost not bring,
Ei tuo he (she) does not bring,
Emme tuo we do not bring,
Ette tuo you (pl.) do not bring,
Evät tuo they do not bring,
En tuonut I did not bring,
Ei tuonut thou didst not bring, etc., which should all be sym-
bolized $\left\{ S \ v^n \right\} V$.

Next, a great many grammatical things are not symbolized :
Number : whether *king* or *kings*, etc.
Tense : whether *comes* or *came, has come* or *will come*, etc.
Person : whether *I*, or *you*, or *he*, or *they*, etc.
Gender or sex : whether *king* or *queen, he* or *she, der tisch* or *die
liebe*, etc.
Degrees of comparison : whether *big* or *bigger* or *biggest*.

Further the symbols disregard the ordinary division into *word-
classes* (*parts of speech*) ; S may be a substantive or a pronoun or
an adjective or an infinitive or a whole clause, and similarly with
O, *O*, P, R, 3, etc.

Here, however, we have two noteworthy exceptions, the Finite
Verb (V), which plays the most important part in the building up of
the most usual type of sentences, and the Preposition (p), which has
likewise a special part to perform ; which justifies the separate symbolization. It may, of course, also be said that by providing the
symbols I for Infinitive and G for Gerund we have stepped outside
the principle of not having separate symbols for the "parts of speech",
but they do not, however, constitute "parts of speech," but like V are
included on account of their syntactic value.

Finally we must say with some emphasis that as the purport of
the system is to provide *general* syntactic symbols, it follows that
forms as such have no place in the system. A purely formal element
is in so far included, as the symbols follow the order in which the
various items occur in the analyzed sentences, and word-order of
course is formal in character. But nothing is said of the significance,
if any, of the word-order, whether in the language analyzed it serves
to show what is Subject, and what Object, etc. It may also be held
that the admission of Infinitive and Gerund constitutes a breach of the
principle here mentioned, as they may be considered forms. But without

them our analysis would have been incomplete and really futile, and their inclusion serves to bring home to us the incontestable truth that in grammar as elsewhere form and matter, outer and inner, cannot be rigidly separated: however much we may try to speak of pure syntax as apart from morphology (accidence), considerations of form will necessarily force themselves on us here and there.

CHAPTER 29.

Form - Function - Notion.

29. 1. Morpheme.

After thus discarding various things in grammar which find no place in our symbolology it will be well to look at a diagram found in PhilGr, p. 56. It contains in three columns, superscribed (A) Form, (B) Function, (C) Notion, one example, the English preterit:

A	B	C
-ed (*handed*)		past time
-t (*fixed*)		unreality in present time (if we *knew*; I wish we *knew*)
-d (*showed*)	preterit	future time (it is time you *went* to bed)
-t with inner change (*left*)		shifted present time (how did you know I *was* a Dane?)
kernel unchanged (*put*)		all times (men *were* deceivers ever).
inner change (*drank*)		
different kernel (*was*)		

Let us look at each of these columns separately and the terminology to be used for each.

Linguistic science has of late years been extremely fertile in new technical terms, but unfortunately there has been no real agreement as to the exact meaning to be ascribed to some of them, even if one and the same term is used by various scholars. There has been a lively discussion on the word *phoneme*, but that is outside the scope of this volume. *Morpheme*, however, must be mentioned here because it would be used by many linguists with regard to column A.

To Noreen (perhaps the first to use the term) *dreieck* and *drei-seitige gradlinige figur* are each of them one morpheme, but these two morphemes mean the same thing and are therefore one and the same sememe.

Marouzeau: élément de formation propre à conférer un aspect grammatical aux éléments de signification; this may be an isolated word (preposition, etc.), but generally the term is used for "éléments de formation qui s'ajoutent à la partie fondamentale du mot".

Vendryes: morpheme is a linguistic element which expresses the relation between the ideas, thus the syllables or sounds added to the root to show the role in the sentence; also the vowel-change in *man : men,* in some languages accent and word-order; he and other French grammarians recognize a "morphème zéro", e.g. in the plural *sheep.*

The Prague Cercle de Linguistique (4.321) : unité morphologique non-susceptible d'être divisée en unités morphologiques plus petites, c'est-à-dire une partie de mot qui, dans toute une série de mots, se présente avec la même fonction formelle et qui n'est pas susceptible d'être divisée en parties plus petites possédant cette qualité.

Bloomfield (Language) : morpheme is the smallest meaningful unit (lexically); he recognizes in "Poor John ran away" five morphemes: *poor, John, ran, a-* and *way.* "The total stock of morphemes in a language is its lexicon".

Zipf (Psycho-Biology of Language 15) reckons as morphemes prefixes, roots, suffixes and endings; in *un-tru-th-ful-ness* we have five morphemes.

Firth (Speech 49) seems to reckon among morphemes only prefixes and suffixes.

J. R. Aiken (New Plan of English Grammar) : morpheme is an empty word which plays the same role as a flexional ending—a suffix thus is no morpheme.

Thus, according to the writer whose definition we prefer, we have to say that *untruthfulness* is one morpheme, or five, or four morphemes. According to one *drank* is one indivisible morpheme, according to someone else, the vowel *a,* which makes this preterit distinct from the infinitive, is a morpheme, but what then is *dr-nk?* And if I exclude the "root" or "stem" from being called a morpheme, am I to say that in the three plurals *wishes, locks, screws,* in which the sound changes automatically according to the final sound of the "root", the ending is one and the same morpheme or three different morphemes? And if the same three forms occur again as the third person singular of the corresponding verbs, is that again the same or a different morpheme? What about *knives,* in which the final sound of the "root" is changed as against the singular *knife?* Is it [z] or the change of [f] to [v] + added [z] that is here the morpheme? Or the whole form *knives?* And when English plural forms are used for the genitive as well as for the "common case" (for the orthographic trick of adding an apostrophe has of course no real linguistic value)— are we to say that we have here added to the common case plural a "morphème zéro"? I can see no way out of these and other diffi- culties except the simple one of avoiding altogether the use of so polysemous a word as morpheme.

For it is, indeed, curious that no such term as morpheme is wanted to describe what is placed in column A: "form" and "change of form" together with a precise indication such as "ending so and so", "vowel change", "the preposition so and so", "word-order" are quite sufficient and have been found so by all grammarians up till quite recent times.

The term *formans* used by Brugmann (IF 14.1, Kurze vgl. gramm. 285) seems to me much better than *morpheme,* as it can never be applied to the ready word, but only to affixes (prefixes, infixes, suffixes) ; but even then there are some terminological difficulties : is *a* in *drank* (or the vowel-change *i/a*) a formans? Is word-order, is an "empty word" a formans?

As a complementary term opposed to morpheme grammarians use the word *sememe* or *semanteme* ; but the meaning of this seems also, though to a lesser degree, to be fluctuating according to the authors using it.

29. 2. Morphoseme.

The name "Function" chosen by me for column B is not very good, as this word is used outside the linguistic world in so vague and comprehensive a way that it is not fit to be used in the science of language in a special technical meaning as opposed to column C "Notion". As a matter of fact much or all of what is placed in C would be reckoned as "function" by most scholars. In column B we have the meeting-ground of outer and inner—but this meeting is the essential characteristic of all linguistic activity, and column B might therefore be superscribed "linguistic centre" or "linguo-centre": what we meet there are units which, as I said, Janus-like face both ways, towards form, and towards notion. A new word seems to be wanted, and I venture to propose **Morphoseme:** I should define a morphoseme as a linguistic unit standing at the intersecting point, where form and notion meet. A morphoseme may have one form, but generally has two or more forms; similarly it corresponds generally not to one notional idea only, but to several. It belongs to one definite language alone.

I have already given one example, the English preterit; other examples of morphosemes are
(1) the Latin genitive, ending now in *-ae,* now in *-i,* now in *-is,* now in *-rum,* etc., and having the various uses (notional meanings) enumerated in grammars: possessive, partitive, definitive, subjective, etc. Thus each case in each particular language is a morphoseme;
(2) the English plural of substantives and pronouns, ending in *-s,* in *-en,* formed by means of vowel-change, irregularly in *we, these, those,* etc. As for notion, this morphoseme more than most approaches to having only one notion, namely 'more-than-one'; still, a perusal of Ch. IV of my Grammar Vol. II will show that even this comparatively simple phenomenon presents "blurred outlines", as linguistic phenomena are apt to;
(3) the English definite article, having in print one form only, though in sound it has at least three; notionally the scheme is much more complicated;
(4) the German definite article, formally greatly varied, *der, den, dem, die,* etc.; notionally almost as the English, but with a great many differences in detail;
(5) the English superlative—but French has no superlative morphoseme, though it is of course capable of expressing the superlative notion.[1]
And so we might go on, but what is said will, I hope, suffice to give a clear idea of what this new term is meant to stand for. I only want to add that the term is useful also in being applicable to lexical units. In a dictionary we treat together as "one word" various "para-

---

[1] This is what was meant by the remark in PhilGr p. 49, which some critics have challenged, as they have overlooked the supplementary remarks on the superlative idea, p. 245.

digmatic" forms, e.g. Lat. *homo, hominem, homini, hominis, homines, hominum, hominibus*; nay, we even put together what Osthoff in a famous book calls "Suppletivwesen". As examples may serve the verb *be* in our languages, English *am, is, was* ... ; *good, better, best,* and correspondingly in other languages; Lat. *fero, tuli, latum.*

A variety of meanings corresponds to each of these units, as a look into any big dictionary will show; but these have nothing in themselves to do with the formal variety of stems making up the paradigm. In fact, one of the most surprising features of linguistic psychology is the development of units, which are felt as such, though neither from the outer nor from the inner point of view there would seem to be a priori any real unity. But the way in which such grammatical and lexical morphosemes come into existence, is outside the scope of this little critical paper.

29. 3. Notion, Extralingual and Intralingual.

If finally we turn to column C "Notion" we shall find that this is not wholly homogeneous. Some of the "notions" are what may be called *extralingual,* i.e. concern things or distinctions which may be observed in the world independently of their linguistic expression. In the example given in the diagram, **29**.1, the difference between past and future time (and "all times") is thus extralingual, and the same may be said of "unreality": "if we knew", etc. But when the preterit is used for "the shifted present time" in indirect speech this cannot in the same way be said to refer to something outside the linguistic expression: it is *intralingual.* If we take other morphosemes as examples, we find similarly that they refer sometimes, but not always, to something extralingual: the distinction between singular and plural corresponds to the outside distinction between one and several individuals of the same species; but in the case of, say, the German or Latin masculine the correspondence with the extralingual quality "male sex" is far from being pure: here the extralingual and the intralingual are inextricably mingled.

29. 4. Meaning of Our Symbols.

If with these considerations in mind we inspect the categories denoted by the symbols exemplified in Part I of the present work, we shall see that only Infinitive (I), Gerund (G), Nexus-substantive (X), Agent-substantive and Participle (Y), Active (ᵃ) and Passive (ᵇ), and possibly negation (ⁿ) can be called morphosemes as being points of intersection between form and notion. Further that *all the symbols denote something purely intralingual*: they have nothing directly to do with the outside world. All of them serve to indicate the *interrelation of linguistic units*[1] *in connected speech* to build up

(a) composite members of a sentence: this is to a great extent done by means of the numerals, and
(b) sentences: this is chiefly done by means of the initial letters.

CHAPTER 30.

Case.

30. 1. Recent Treatments.

In view of the definition just given it might be questioned if I should not in my symbols have provided signs for cases, as these admittedly serve to show the interrelations of words in a sentence. I am, however, quite certain that I have done well in not including case symbols; in order to justify this exclusion it will be necessary to devote some pages to the theory of grammatical cases. Cf. Linguistica, p. 322 ff. (System of Grammar, p. 23 ff.)

In a recently published first part of a big work L. Hjelmslev deals with the notion of case in general and the most important ancient and modern treatments of the subject: "La Catégorie des Cas. Étude de Grammaire Générale" (Acta Jutlandica VII, publ. by the University of Aarhus). On the first page the author says: "L'analyse grammaticale doit commencer par l'analyse des cas. Il n'y a peut-être pas de catégorie grammaticale dont l'aspect immédiat soit si clair, si cohérent, si symétrique, si facilement abordable que celle des cas". This is, to my mind, a serious misstatement: as appears clearly from the author's own book, there is nothing clear, symmetrical and easily accessible in the case systems actually found in different languages: otherwise the numerous diverging theories and explana-

---

[1] By linguistic units are here meant parts of words, words, or groups of words.

tions of grammarians would be totally incomprehensible, and I think we get nearer the truth by emphasizing what Hjelmslev himself says in the very next sentence, viz. that "le système des cas est dans bon nombre de langues d'une complexité énorme, posant à la fois tous les problèmes de la grammaire".

Hjelmslev has not considered the recent attempt at a comprehensive case-theory (for the Indo-European languages) due to Max Deutschbein (see Atti del III Congresso Internazionale dei Linguisti, Roma, sett. 1933, p. 141 ff.). A few words on his system will not be out of place here. The chief cases are characterized as follows:

a. Dynamische kohärenz: akkusativ,
b. Kinetische kohärenz: dativ,
c. Statische kohärenz: genitiv.

In *a* we have "verbindung der sphären von A und B", in *b* "verknüpfung", in *c* "verschmelzung". On the other hand we have:

a unterordnung; B wird A untergeordnet: akkusativ.
b nebenordnung:
  B wird A zugeordnet: dativ.
  B ist A beigeordnet: instrumentalis.
  B ist mit A zusammengeordnet: soziativus.
c einordnung: B ist A eingeordnet: genitiv.
d ausordnung: B wird (ist) von A ausgeordnet: ablativ.

To the very just critical remarks pronounced by scholars of various nations in Rome I should like to add that the whole of this system seems to be built up exclusively on the basis of expressions peculiar to the German language and found in exactly the same way in no other language, chiefly compounds with *ordnung*. Nor are the ideas expressed by the prepositions and prefixes entering into these compounds, *unter, neben, zu, bei, zusammen, ein, aus,* sufficiently clear and definite to allow a perfectly logical structure such as Deutschbein imagines. It would be impossible to translate the system, e.g., into French or English. Even to a German pupil these expressions and explanations would be of very little help indeed, if he were placed before the task of understanding or of employing the cases of any language whatever. Nothing is gained by twisting grammar into such an artificial framework.

There is a valuable paper by F. R. Blake, "A Semantic Analysis of Case" in the Curme Volume (*Language Monographs* No. 7. 1930). But it deals exclusively with what the writer understands by

Case, i.e. the notional ideas underlying case in the widest sense of
that word, and not with what he calls *case form*, which is just what
is meant in this paper by case. Thus he has, e.g., among his "im-
material adnominal cases" descriptive (a man *of the sea*), contentive
(a cup *of water*), mensural (a period *of two weeks*), additional (four
boys *besides the man*), etc., etc. The whole gives rather what I should
call a survey of the possible uses of prepositions, etc. The writer
claims, with some justification, that the majority of all essential case
relations are listed in his scheme, and that it is in its main outlines
of universal application. The same is claimed by A. Noreen for his
scheme of "status",[1] which Blake does not know, and with which it
would be interesting to compare it in detail—a task which, however,
lies totally outside the scope of my book.

Paul's golden words of 1910, which I quoted in *Phil. of Grammar*[2] 186, still hold good: "Die kasus sind nur ausdrucksmittel, die
nicht zum notwendigen bestande jeder sprache gehören, die da, wo
sie vorhanden sind, nach den verschiedenen sprachen und ent-
wickelungsstufen mannigfach variieren, und von denen man nicht
erwarten darf, dass sich ihre funktionen mit konstanten logischen oder
psychologischen verhältnissen decken" (Zeitschr. f. psych. 1910,
114).

30. 2. Latin.

To give a concrete illustration of this view of cases in general,
I shall now give a short survey of the way in which the cases actually
found in two distinct languages, are used, as shown by a "translation"
into my own symbols.

Nominative.

S (including S = O [a] in a passive sentence).
P (including P in such a passive sentence as Numa creatus est rex,
                    cf. creaverunt Numan regem; cf. the symbol
                              $\frac{1}{2}$ above Ch. **16**).

---

[1] See Vårt språk, vol. V; Noreen-Pollak, Wiss. betrachtung der spr. 345 ff.

[2] My "Final Words about Cases" (ib. p. 185—6) ought, in conformity with
the arrangement in other chapters, to have been placed in the beginning of
the chapter on Cases.—There are some very valuable remarks on cases and
their relation to gender (animate and inanimate) in two papers by H. V.
Velten, in Language 8.255 ff. and BSL 33.2.205 ff., but they deal to a
great extent with pre-history and history and thus fall outside the scope of
my present work.

Accusative.

O (including O^r) with V.

O rarely with X: quid tibi hanc tactio est?

O or [ ] ("cognate object") : tutiorem vitam vivere.

two O: docet me litteras V O O$_2$, or V *O* O.

    Caesarem sententiam rogaverunt O O$_2$ V.

O with a passive: Caesar sententiam rogatus est S O V^b.

S and P as parts of nexus as object:

    Avaritia homines caecos reddit S O^r(S$_2$ P) V.

    Dicit eam esse felicem V O(S I P).

S and P in exclamations: Me miserum! S P!

O or S (?) : pudet regem facti, possibly V O/S O.

1 after some prepositions: ad (per, in, etc.) urbem: p1.

3 in many ways: Roman (domum) ire, hasta sex pedes longa,
                viginti annos vixit, id temporis, etc.[1]

Dative.

O : do tibi librum$\left\{SV\right\}$ *O* O. Thus also in : hunc mihi terrorem eripe.

O, where there is only one object: nocet hosti, praeest exercitui,
      cedant arma togae. Or, should we here, too, write *O*? **36.7.**

O/S: tibi invidetur.

P: Hoc nobis detrimento erit S R P V.

R: puero est nomen Marcus / Sex nobis filii sunt / civis reipublicae
                utilis / quod licet Jovi.[2]

But how to symbolize: tibi est pugnandum? *O*(S) V G, or R(S) V G.

Ablative.

2 (descriptive) : mulier eximia pulchritudine 12(21).

P (descriptive) : Cicero tanta eloquentia est S P(21) V.

S and P in dependent nexus: Cicerone consule, rege interfecto, me
                invito 3(SP).

3/O might perhaps be written in: utor victoria, gaudeo vino, otio
           egeo, though O is sufficiently clear.

3 in a great many different employments: nullo modo, ira incitatus,

---

[1] All these must from a synchronic point of view be considered distinct employments of one and the same case, though it may be possible to derive them all from analogous extensions of the notion of direction, as Bréal has attempted to do, Essai de Sémantique, 1897, p. 245 ff.

[2] Donat coronas suis V O O = donat suos coronis V O 3 ; cf. Eng. present crowns to one's friends = present one's friends with crowns.

non re sed nomine, Athenis vivit, tertio anno, multis
annis ante, Cicerone eloquentior, aeger pedibus, etc.
1 after some prepositions: ab, cum, ex, in, etc.

Genitive.

O : memini (obliviscor) sceleris $\left\{SV\right\}$ O.

Poenitet me consilii (probably best) V S O.

Accuso eum furti $\left\{SV\right\}$ O O$_2$, or $\left\{SV\right\}$ O 3.

1^2 : patris domus 1^21, hostis Romanorum 11^2.
S^2 : amor matris, timor hostium XS^2.
O^2 : amor filii, timor hostium XO^2; patiens laboris YO^2.

Thus also with *avidus, cupidus, peritus,* etc.

1 or 1$^{(2)}$ after quantifier: pars militum, quid novi, uterque eorum,
multum temporis, satis pecuniae 2^{q}1, cf. **32**.4.

(But: uterque frater, utraque castra 2^{q}1.)
Vir summae virtutis $11(21)^2$.

[ ]: vox voluptatis 1 [1].

Here the genitive is used to avoid placing two substantives in
the same case together: such juxtaposition is allowed only when a
common name qualifies a proper name: urbs Roma. Cf. above
4.4.

3 : Romae vivit 3 V.

30. 3. Finnish.[1]

Nominative.

S and P: pojat ovat iloiset 'the boys are glad'. It is noteworthy that
the nominative as S is used only if the idea is definite, so that
pojat means 'the boys'; cf. partitive.

S in a so-called "passive" sentence is really an O: koira ajetaan
huoneesta ulos 'the dog is sent out of the room'.

S in a dependent nexus: Pojat seisovat kädet lanteilla 'the boys
stand hands on hips' S V 3(S$_2$ 3); mies makaa pää paljaana 'the
man is lying with his head bare' S V 3(S$_2$ P).

---

[1] The examples are taken from E. N. Setälä, Finska språkets satslära (2. ed.
Helsingfors 1903) and C. N. E. Eliot, A Finnish Grammar (Oxford 1890).

Genitive.

1^2: pojan kirja 'the boy's book' $1^2 1$.

S^2: leivon laulu 'the skylark's song (singing)' $S^2 X$.

O^2: isänmaan rakkaus 'fatherland's love', 'love of native country', kaupungin valloittaminen 'the conquest of the town' $O^2 X$. (Where there is a subjective genitive, O is expressed in other ways: kansalaisen rakkaus isänmaata kohtaan (partitive) 'the citizen's love of the native country', isän toiveet pojasta (elative) 'the father's hope with regard to his son' $S^2 XO$).

[ ]: Helsingin kaupunki 'the town of Helsingfors'; Imatran koski 'the waterfall of Imatra' [1] 1.

Accusative.

O, but only if the idea is definite: isä ostaa kirjan pojalle 'the father buys the book for the boy' S V O O.

P as part of an O: räätäli teki takin liian lyhyen 'the tailor made the coat too short' S V $O^r(13P)$.

3 to express duration of time, how many times, etc.

Partitive.

S (indefinite): lihaa on pöydällä '(some) meat is on the table, there is meat on the table' S V 3.

O (indefinite): emäntä leikkasi lapsille lihaa 'the housewife cut (some) meat for the children' S V O O, poika lukee kirjaa 'the boy is reading the book'; in a negative sentence the O is always in the partitive: poika ei antanut kirjaa 'the boy did not give the book' S v^n V O.

P: Varpuset ovat lintuja 'sparrows (nom., all sparrows) are birds (some of the birds, belong to the class of birds) S V P, pojat ovat iloisia 'boys are happy', sormus on kultaa 'the ring is (of) gold', isolated in exclamations: kauheaa 'horrible!'

After a quantifier: naula lihaa 'a pound of meat' $2^q 1$, paljo rahaa 'much money'.

3 in various ways, i.a. as second member of comparison.

Essive.

P: isä on pappina 'the father is a clergyman' S V P, hän oli minulla apuna 'he (she) was to me a help' S V R P.

P in a nexus: pitää jotakin häpeänä 'think a thing a shame' V O(S P).

[ ]: Poika palasi alakuloisena koulusta 'the boy came-back dejected from school' S V [2] 3, poikana hän oli kokonaan toisenlainen 'as a boy he was totally different' [1] S 3 P.
3 to denote a definite period of time.

Translative.

P[r]: Isä on jo tullut vanhaksi 'the father has now grown old' S v 3 V P[r], Niilo rupesi sotamieheksi 'N. became a soldier', hän tuli minulle avuksi 'he (she) came to my assistance', he valitsivat hänet puhujaksi 'they chose him as spokesman' S V O[r](S_2 P), hän sanoi sinua varkaaksi 'he called you a thief', kaupunki paloi tuhaksi 'the town was burnt to ashes' S V P[r].
Here we have the characteristic expression: äiti makasi lapsensa kuoliaaksi 'the mother lay her child (into) dead (overlay it)' S V O[r](S_2 P).
Various related uses: Hän on sopiva puhujaksi 'he is clever as a speaker' S V P [1], emäntä teki valmistuksia jouluksi 'the housewife made preparations for the Christmas (yule)'.
3, tertiary of time and manner.

Allative.

O : äiti antoi kirjan pojallensa 'the mother gave her boy a book' S V O O.
R: hän oli minulla apuna 'he was a help to me' S V R P.
3 : chiefly movement on to or into the neighbourhood of something.

The other Finnish cases need not occupy us here, they are chiefly local and stand in the sentence as 3. The Finnish cases were first arranged in a complete system by Rask (see his Udvalgte afhandlinger II. 258) ; this system as rearranged by Hjelmslev (Catég. des Cas 64) looks thus:

I	II	III	IV
nominative	accusative	allative	illative
genitive	essive	adessive	inessive
partitive	abessive	ablative	elative

Here the uppermost line is said to indicate a movement to, the middle one rest, and the third, movement from; the difference between I, II, etc., denotes in principle various degrees of intimacy. But, as Hjelmslev justly remarks, even in a system so evidently localistic as the Finnish there is no purely local case "dans le sens concret, massif et matériel du terme. Même les cas qui se prêtent le plus facilement à cet emploi remplissent en même temps un rôle purement syntagmatique ou "logique".

30. 4. Comparison.

Things thus are seen to be less rectilinear in the actual world than would appear from the tabulation above; and as we find similar diversities in the use of cases in most (or all?) of the languages that have cases at all, it would seem difficult, not to say impossible, to fulfil the requirement expressed by Hjelmslev (p. 85): "Un cas, comme une forme linguistique en général, ne signifie pas plusieurs choses différentes; il signifie une seule chose, il porte une seule notion abstraite dont on peut déduire les emplois concrets". This at most can be an ideal put before the investigator, who should always try, wherever possible, to discover unity behind diversity of the phenomena.

In neither of the two languages specially considered here do we find either the same case used everywhere for the same purpose or the same syntactic category (as expressed in our symbols S, P, O, etc.) denoted always by the same case. When some grammarians speak of the cases nominative, accusative, dative, and genitive, as the four purely "grammatical" or "logical" cases as contrasted with "local" cases, they are forced to admit that not a single language in the world possesses this simple system in its purity.

As I have said on several occasions, we should not, in treating of the grammar of any language, recognize more cases, or other cases, than are clearly distinguished by formal criteria; thus we have no dative in English or Danish, no ablative in Greek, etc. A case is always a "*morphoseme*" in the sense defined above. As a matter of fact we rarely have one form only, and as rarely one notional use only; generally several forms go together to produce one case, which again serves to express more than one notion. Where thus several form-classes meet with several notional classes there is never the slightest correspondence between any one of the A-divisions and any one of the C-divisions. Sometimes historical grammar is capable of pointing out how formerly distinct units coalesced in course of time into one ("syncretism"), but this serves only to put into relief the universal tendency mentioned above (**29**.2) towards the creation of "morphosemes" consisting of disparate formal and notional elements.

As Sechehaye says (Structure logique, p. 74) "Il est bien certain que, même si la langue dispose d'un jeu de distinctions [casuelles] relativement riche, ce jeu ne recouvrira que d'une façon bien imparfaite l'infinie variété des relations possibles. Le procédé flexionnel a donc des limites".

30. 5. Genitive.

As matters stand thus it is impossible in a system like ours to find any place for cases. The only case one could think of providing a sign for would be the genitive, but then it should not be for all the varied uses of that case in any of the actually existing languages, but only for that use which may be considered the central and relatively most indispensable one in those languages that do possess such a case, namely the one found in *John's house, wife, servants, master, enemies, life, opinions, works, books* (in two senses), *portrait*, etc.— indicating not only "possession", but any kind of intimate relation. Though this definition seems rather vague,[1] it is really more definite than most of the case relations denoted in Indo-European and other languages. Still it falls outside the frame of our system : there is, however, one circumstance which calls for symbolization in this use of the genitive, namely that it changes the word from being a primary into a secondary by making it an adjunct of the item with which it

---

[1] This vagueness is the basis of some quibbles (in Plato) of the Greek sophists : Have you got a dog? has this dog young ones? then the dog is a father; but as it is yours, it must consequently be your father.—Your ox is an ox which you may sell or kill, etc. But now if you recognize Zeus as your god, have you the same power over him?—The difficulty is solved when we see that the genitive merely denotes close relationship, but that the relationship naturally varies according to the two (persons or things) that are connected by means of the genitive.

is combined. This is what we denote by the raised ^{2}; *John's (my) house* is written 1^21, which really amounts to the same thing as 21. Cf. the use of the symbols S^2 and O^2 in Chs. **19, 20, 21.** [1]

CHAPTER 31.

Rank.

31. 1. General Theory.

Since I first started my theory of Rank (1913) I have had occasion several times to revert to it,[2] and, thanks to some extent to the criticisms of other scholars, I hope I have gradually clarified this fascinating theme by eliminating doubts and bringing new facets to light. The elaboration of my system of symbols has made me take up the subject again and has made me see a few things in a new light, though the main features of the theory have remained exactly as they were from the beginning. I hope I may therefore be forgiven for here briefly restating my view, trying to avoid some of the less felicitous expressions and examples used in former expositions.

There are two series which to some extent, but only to some extent, run parallel; I call them α and β. In α we have separate classes of words (parts of speech), in β separate ranks, thus

α. Word-Classes:	β. Ranks:
Substantives	Primaries (1)
Adjectives	Secondaries (2)
Adverbs	Tertiaries (3).

---

[1] With regard to case attention may finally be called to two opposite tendencies in the development of languages: one towards using the nominative for S and P even in dependent position (*he being dead*, Sp. similarly *yo*; nominative after preposition in the cases exemplified in **9**.5; Portuguese *eu* with a dependent infinitive, the English use with the gerund, G. "lassen den grafen dieser gesandte sein", etc.)—and the other towards making position prevail over notion: it is me, Dan. det er mig, F. c'est lui, G. dial. er ist einen schönen mann, etc. See also PhilGr 118, 338.

[2] Sprogets logik, 1913, p. 28 ff., Modern English Grammar II, 1914, p. 2 ff., The Philosophy of Grammar, 1924, p. 96 ff., Englische Studien, 60, 1926, p. 300 ff., Essentials of English Grammar, 1933, Ch. VIII.

The chief, and extremely important, distinction between the two series is this, that in α we deal with isolated words in their dictionary or lexical value, while in β we deal not only with words, but also with combinations of words (wortgefüge), and we take both of these as they appear in connected speech. We can look up words in a dictionary and there find that *happiness* is a substantive, *happy* an adjective, and *happily* an adverb, but the dictionary can never tell us whether a word or a group of words in one particular connexion stands as a primary, as a secondary or as a tertiary. That can only be decided by means of a syntactic analysis of the whole combination in which it occurs.

In Saussurean phrase we may say that α belongs to *la langue,* and β to *la parole.*

In the easiest and simplest cases the two series cover one another, thus

	terribly	cold	weather
α	adverb	adjective	substantive
β	tertiary	secondary	primary.

But this simple parallelism does not always hold good. Both substantives and adverbs may under certain circumstances be secondaries; adjectives and adverbs are sometimes primaries; one and the same combination of words, even a whole clause, can be used in each of the three ranks.

Plenty of examples of this are found in my previous books, in the most easily accessible way in Essentials of Engl. Grammar. Many illustrations are also found in Part I of this treatise.

31. 2. Quaternaries, etc.

The parallelism between word-classes and ranks is further seen to be deficient through the fact that while in α we have only three classes, in β it is possible to lengthen the series of numerals, as in *a not* (5) *particularly* (4) *well* (3) *constructed* (2) *plot* (1), in which *constructed* qualifies *plot, well* qualifies *constructed,* and so on backwards, while we have no "part of speech" which bears the same relation to an adverb as this does to an adjective: in the example chosen here *not, particularly,* and *well* are equally adverbs.[1]

In PhilGr, p. 96, I expressly mention the possibility of having quaternaries, quinaries, and so forth, but say that "it is needless to distinguish more than three ranks, as there are no formal or other traits that distinguish words of these lower orders from tertiary words". What I meant was that there was no need for distinct *terms,* though on p. 97 I say that "quaternary words, in the rare cases in which a special name is needed, may be termed sub-subjuncts". In the present scheme numerals are all that is wanted. Nor is the term formerly used by me, *adnex* for a secondary in a nexus, necessary when the symbols are used: it means V in "the horse runs", I in "we saw the horse run", and P in "I thought her happy".

31. 3. Specializing.

The expression used in PhilGr, p. 96, to explain the rank system, "different ranks of words according to their mutual relation as defining or defined" is better than that used immediately before, that "there is one word (should be word or part of a word or group of words) of supreme importance to which the others are joined as subordinates". It is not intrinsic importance that is decisive, but only grammatical importance, and, as further elaborated in PhilGr, this depends in a junction chiefly on the interrelation as specialized and specializing: *a secondary specifies (specializes) its primary, and a tertiary specifies the secondary,* (or the primary as specified by the secondary).

It seems obvious that the word "specifies" implies 'specifies the *idea* expressed by' and not the word as such, which cannot of course be made more special than it is. I say this expressly here, because it is sometimes necessary to obviate even the most unreasonable criticism.

These terms, specializing and specialized (specifying and specified, defining and defined, determining and determined, restrictive and

---

[1] On the other hand it must be admitted that the corresponding example previously used by me, "a certainly not very cleverly worded remark", was not very cleverly devised, for *certainly* does not in the same way qualify *not* as each of the other words qualifies the word immediately following it; the symbolization must be 32(5432)1, *certainly* qualifying the whole of the composite secondary *not very cleverly worded.* We might even write <3> for *certainly.*

restricted) seem to cover the relation in ordinary junctions: *a hat* without any adjunct stands for something more vague, thus also more comprehensive than *a black hat* or *John's hat* or *my hat*. There are more hats in existence than black hats or hats belonging to John or to me.[1]

There are, however, exceptions in which an adjunct has no such restrictive function. In a caressing exclamation "My dear little Mary!" the speaker intends no contrast either to someone else's Mary or to a less beloved or bigger Mary. But that changes nothing with regard to what occupies us here: the symbolization must remain the same: 1^2221. Just as speakers do not always scruple to extend the meaning of an individual word outside its "proper sphere", they have in such cases employed the grammatical category adjective-adjunct + substantive-primary in a widened sense. Other examples: "cruel Iago", "der treffliche Rathenau". Thus also "the white snow", which must be written like "the white dress" although not used in contrast with an impossible black or red snow. This symbolization is a simple consequence of what has been stated emphatically above: our symbols have nothing to do with the meaning of words as such. (On restrictive and non-restrictive adjuncts see PhilGr 108, 111).

31. 4. Coordination.

Coordination is found, not only when it is expressly indicated as in

John and Mary came S_1 & S_2 V;

They are married and happy S V P_1 & P_2;

They are married, but unhappy S V P_1 & P_2 (the distinction between *and* and *but* is irrelevant for our purpose)—

---

[1] The point of view here advanced is only indirectly connected with my theory that substantives are generally more special than adjectives. As the formulas dealt with in this volume are independent of word-classes as such, I need not repeat what I said on the subject in PhilGr, but will only stress the fact that I did not give this view as universally true; cf. p. 75 "not always and under all circumstances", 79 "the numerical test cannot always be applied", 81 "broadly distinguished". Sonnenschein could not justly argue against me such an example as "carnivorous animals": there are more animals than carnivores! Quite so, but *carnivorous* means 'flesh-eating': the adjectival element is *eating*, and that applies to more beings than animals. In *flesh-eating* (*carnivorous*) the secondary element is specialized in the same way as when it is accompanied by a tertiary.

but also very frequently without such express indication. Combinations like *Peter, John and Mary came* should be symbolized S_1 &⁰ S_2 & S_3 V, where &⁰ means that there is no *and* expressed. But no symbol is required for such cases of coordination as *He is often there* S V 3 3 with two tertiaries.

Combinations like *Mr. Brown* (11), *Captain John Smith* (111, see Ch. **4**) are also cases of coordination.[1] It cannot be argued against this that a title is less important than, i.e. "subordinate to", the name it precedes, for we are dealing here not with the relative importance in intrinsic meaning, but with grammatical position. Nor does accentual subordination concern us in this connexion; as a matter of fact we may sometimes stress *Mr.* more than *Brown* to bring out the contrast with Miss Brown or Mrs. Brown, and in the second combination we may sometimes stress the three items *Captain, John* and *Smith* equally, and at other times give prominence to one or the other of them, but these variations produce no change in the grammatical rank of the words, and consequently none in our symbolization.

In most cases of apposition, too, we have the same rank (generally 1) in the items thus joined together. Hammerich says that in "Ist sie aber nett, die Amalia" *Amalia* is evidently subordinate to *sie*. I feel they are coordinate, at any rate in the sense here considered. On some special cases to which I am inclined to extend the idea "apposition" (*proud : pride, die : death*) see Ch. **20**.4.

31. 5. Subordination.

Subordination is found first in combinations 21 or 12 as in the extremely frequent collocations of adjective and substantive, *red flag* (21), F. *drapeau rouge* (12), in which the adjective is an adjunct (above Ch. **3**). In the same way we transcribe *those present* 12, but *those ones* and *(the) present ones* 21.

Where there are two or more adjuncts to the same primary it is generally possible to divide them into smaller units, as has been done with "curious little living creatures" in **3**.1; but this has not been

---

[1] I did not see this when in PhilGr, p. 98, I spoke of *Captain* as adjunct to *Smith*, though my parenthetic "why not?" showed a certain hesitancy.

thought necessary in all examples where it would have made parentheses within parentheses necessary.

It is perhaps doubtful whether *home,* etc. in combinations like the following should be recognized as adjuncts. I should transcribe:
on my way home (back) from the office pl($1^212(3pl)$).

G. unser weg nach hause $1^212(pl)$.

Cp. the then government 21, an up-train 3/2-1, etc.

The examples given above (**3**.6 ff.) of irregular junctions are probably self-explanatory. Note that the symbol 2(3)1 is used in **3**.9 in the cases in which a secondary accompanied by a tertiary is raised to a primary, and that this symbolization fits both those cases in which there is no difference between the adverbial and the adjectival form (*die geistig armen*) and those in which the adverbial form is retained (*the mentally deficient; the truly modest;* in philosophical parlance even *the barely possibles,* in which the primary is treated as a substantive). The employment of the symbol 2(3) in compounds like *afterthought* (**6**.4) as contrasted with *afternoon,* in which *after* is a preposition governing the last element, will probably be approved by all.

31. 6. Genitive.

Next, subordination is found in genitival combinations.

As already remarked, there is no separate sign for genitive any more than for other cases, but in the most common employment of this case it shifts the rank from 1, as in the nominative, etc., to 2, and this shifting is denoted by the index ^{2} added either to the numeral 1 or to one of the letters implying primary rank. A combination like *Shakespeare's wisdom* (1^21) is thus, as far as rank is concerned, completely analogous to an adjective-adjunct + substantive-primary: *Shakespearean wisdom* (21). As genitives we must here also regard possessive pronouns: *my hat, his wisdom* ($1^21 = 21$). *Wisdom* of course is X, but that is a primary.

31. 7. Used as Primaries.

When adjectives, genitives, and possessive pronouns, which generally are secondaries, are used as primaries, the notation must be

altered accordingly. The examples given of this in **3**.9 are presumably
clear enough, even without the explanations added within parentheses.
In some languages possessive pronouns have separate forms when
they are primaries: *mine, le mien, der mein(ig)e* must be written
1 or, according to circumstances, S, O, O. In "I bought it at the
butcher's" the last three words together form a tertiary like most
prepositional groups, but *the butcher's* is a primary 1, though we
must symbolize the expanded form *at the butcher's shop* p1(1^21)—
for here, evidently, *the butcher's* is secondary to *shop*.

31. 8. Compounds.

Finally we have subordination in the ordinary type of compound
substantives. The relation of the two members in *silk dress* is evidently
analogous to that in *white dress*: both combinations indicate kinds
of dresses different from *cotton dress* or *black dress*. The symbol for
silk, cotton must therefore be 2 as for *white* and *black*. That the
connexion is closer than in *black dress* is indicated by the hyphen:
silk dress 2-1. Most of the symbolizations of compounds given in
Ch. **6** are self-evident; thus also compounds with the order 1-2
("initialdeterminativen"). As with junctions we must in many cases
of string-compounds dissolve these into minor units, indicated by
means of parentheses, so that compounds which in themselves are 1,
become 2 in relation to something else.

In Ch. **6**.6 we have singled out and denoted separately compounds
like *blackbird* 2+1, in which the first element is an adjective-
adjunct to the second. *Blackbird* 2+1 differs from *black bird* 21
formally through weak stress on *bird,* notionally through a highly
specialized meaning: not all black birds are blackbirds. In *holiday*
we have further a shortening of the first vowel; in *blackberry* the
second vowel is reduced to [ə]: with regard to the meaning note the
old joke: *when blackberries are green* (i.e. not ripe) *they are red.*
In Dan. *gråvær* (*graavejr*) the first vowel is shortened and lowered,
etc. Notionally such compounds are distinct from those of the type
greenhouse, sweetshop, in which the first element is a substantive
(note the plural *greens, sweets*); these thus belong to the ordinary
type 2-1. The same is true of *blacksmith,* which in NED is defined
"a smith who works in iron or black metal, as distinct from a 'white-
smith' who works in tin or white metal"—the smith thus is not black.

On the other hand it must be admitted that there are certain compounds in which it is not possible to recognize a subordination: the two parts are on the same footing (equipollent), exactly as the three elements in *Captain John Smith*. Examples see Ch. **6.**

I think *Tuesday evening* must be put down as 2-1, exactly as *Christmas Eve*, etc.; but what about *this day week*? 213? English is full of such formless collocations which more or less defy analysis.

How to symbolize adjectives like *snow-white*? They are compounds of substantive and adjective, and yet we cannot write them 1-2: in them we once more see clearly that *substantive* is not equal to *primary* and *adjective* is not equal to *secondary,* for the relation is exactly reversed: the first element here, as usual in compounds, is subordinate to the second. Now *snow-white* together is an adjective which usually is an adjunct in which snow is a tertiary; the whole *a snow-white dress* therefore is $2(3\text{-}2)1$.

Genitival compounds $1^2\text{-}1$ are analyzed in **6**.3, where it is shown that *mother's heart* when corresponding to G. *mutterherz* must be symbolized in a different way from the ordinary genitival adjunct.

Under nexus-words, gerunds, etc., further examples of compounds are given.

The orthography of English compounds is so chaotic that nothing can be deduced from the way in which these words are spelt. The same is true, though to a lesser degree, in other languages (Dan. *idag* or *i dag*; Du. *er van* = G. *davon,* etc.): everywhere we run up against the difficulty of deciding what is *one* word and what two or more—a difficulty which no grammarian has been able to get over. (*Is not* = *isn't* I have sometimes written V 3^n, sometimes V^n: let critics call me inconsistent, if they like).

31. 9. Results.

As a final result of my renewed reflexions I must say that I think the theory of rank very useful, even indispensable, in bringing about a clear understanding (and representation) of many important points concerning the interrelation of linguistic units, this in spite of the fact that there remain a certain number of cases in which scholars may perhaps be of different views as to the allotment of the numbers

1, 2 and 3 to definite items. We shall see further difficulties in the chapter on Quantifiers and later in the chapter on Rank in nexus, in both of which we meet with special relations to be taken in consideration different from those in junctions.

It will be well to place together here the symbols for various combinations of *black*.
Black bird 21 = bird characterized by blackness; cf. small bird.
Blackbird 2 + 1 = one particular kind of black bird.
Black-blue dress 2(3-2)1.
A coal-black nigger 2(3-2)1.
Blacksmith 2-1; cf. goldsmith.
Black-and-tans 2(2&2)1°.
Blackshirt 2(21)1° = one wearing a black shirt.
Blackhaired girls 2(21+)1 = characterized by black hair.
Bootblack O-Y or 2(O)-Y.
Dr. Black 11.
Black, the novelist 1 [1].

The regimen of a preposition is everywhere supposed to be a primary except where special relations are to be taken into account; but 1 need not be specially written when the regimen is a simple S, O, *O,* I, G, X or Y without any additions.

CHAPTER 32.

Quantifiers.

32. 1. Quantifier and Quantified.

We find four distinct ways of combining a quantifier, here denoted q, with the quantified item, here Q.
(a) qQ, q as adjective to Q: many girls, five girls.
(b) qQ, q as a substantive: G. ein glas wein, Dan. et glas vin.
(c) qQ^2, different from (b) by Q being in the genitive: L. poculum vini; Ru. stakan vina.
(d) qpQ: a glass of wine, F. un verre de vin.

Now if we try to apply the theory of ranks to such combinations, it is easy to see that the linguistic treatment of them is not always the same: in (a) q is evidently treated as a secondary, Q as a

primary; in (c) and (d) it is inversely q that is treated as the
primary, and Q is expressed in two ways that are generally used for
secondaries. The collocation in (b) shows in itself nothing about the
rank.

32. 2. Difference from Qualifier.

This incongruity in the treatment of quantifiers finds its natural
explanation in the fact that they are different from ordinary (restrictive) adjuncts: while these qualify, i.e. specify, define, a primary,
this is not the case with quantifiers: *nice girls* says something about
the kind of girls, *many girls* speaks only of the number. *Nice girls*
may be paraphrased 'girls who are nice', but no similar paraphrase
is possible with *many girls.* "I saw many nice girls" = "I saw many
girls who were nice", but not = "I saw nice girls who were many".
In such cases where a quantifier and a qualifier are combined, the
former is always placed first. Similarly in "I drank a bottle of good
wine", which in spite of the preposition is parallel with "I drank
much good wine".

32. 3. Partitive.

There seems little doubt that both (c) and (d) originally started
from a partitive idea, (part of a definite quantity) as in L. *pars
militum, multi militum* ; G. *viele unserer freunde* ; Ru. *čast' soldatov ;*
and on the other hand L. *unus ex tribunis, pauci de nostris* ; G. *keiner
von den gegnern, die hälfte von dem silber;* F. *une partie du vin, un
grand nombre de nos amis.* But they were by an easy extension applied
to an indefinite quantity (genitivus generis) as in the examples given
above; in both cases the extended use was promoted by the general
disinclination to an immediate collocation of two substantives in the
same case.[1]

While we have a partitive use in *many of us, three of us,* there
is no partitive idea in *all of us, the three of us,* to which the symbol
for apposition with *of,* was applied above. *A glass of water* might
similarly be written 1^q [p1]; this analysis, however, does not seem
the best.

---

[1] This disinclination is seen also in the appositions mentioned in **4.**4 and in
French constructions like "le livre du grand étymologiste qu'est M. A.
Thomas".

32. 4. Symbols.

Numerals are generally treated as adjectives as in (a), but not infrequently the higher ones or some of them are substantives and require the construction (c) or (d) ; in Ru. even from 5 upwards. In English we have *a hundred soldiers, a million inhabitants, a dozen bottles,* but *hundreds of soldiers, millions of inhabitants, dozens of bottles*; in a similar way the Romans said *mille milites,* but *duo milia militum.*

Are these now to be treated differently in our system? Should *mille milites* be written 2^q1, but *duo milia militum* 2^q11^2 (or $2^q1^q 1^2$)? Should the notation in Russian change suddenly in the beginning of the series of numerals from 2^q1 to 1^q1^2? Further, if we write *a dozen bottles* like *twelve bottles,* is it not a little strange to treat *dozens of bottles* in another way? After a good deal of hesitation I have finally adopted the plan of *everywhere taking the quantifier as secondary and the quantified as primary,* no matter how expressed. This is nothing but a consistent carrying out of the general principle of disregarding form and penetrating behind it to the notional (or, if you like, the logical) kernel of the matter.[1]

As it is always prudent to leave open a back-door, I may for the benefit of those who should object to writing *poculum vini* 2^q1 without indication of case, recommend the symbolization $2^q1^{(2)}$ so as to show that *vini* is in the genitive without having the ordinary value of a genitive.

If we write *a dozen bottles* 2^q1 (and in the same way Dan. *en snes æg* 'a score of eggs' 2^q1), the natural consequence is to use the same symbol for G. *ein glas wein,* Dan. *et glas vin.* Some Danish scholars, with whom I discussed the matter would write 21, others inversely 12, just as there is a good deal of vacillation among those of my countrymen who write primaries with a capital, whether to write *Alt godt* or *alt Godt.* Germans write *nichts Neues* as if *nichts* were an adjective and *neues* a substantive ; in English we say *nothing new* as 12, originally 2^q12, and in French it is *rien de vrai* 2^qpl, originally $12(\text{pl})$. All this goes to show the difficulty of applying the theory of ranks outside of qualifiers.[2]

---

[1] Sweet says (NEG § 120) : "The nucleus of the group *a piece of bread* is *bread,* for *piece,* although grammatically the head word of the group, is really little more than a form-word". I may adduce this in favour of my notation $2^q1(\text{pl})$, though Sweet does not speak of quantifier.

[2] I have everywhere written *no* as 2^q, not as 2^n or 2^{nq}.

CHAPTER 33.

Nexus.

33. 1. Predication.

After dealing with various kinds of junction we shall now consider the other kind of syntactic combination, nexus. While junction is regularly symbolized by a collocation of figures: 21 good boy, 12 fee simple, 11 King Edward, 2-1 picture-gallery, 2 + 1 blackberry, 1-1 boy messenger, etc., the most characteristic symbol for a nexus is the presence of one or generally two or more of the initials: S V he drank, S V P he became happy, S V O he had a drink, S V $O^r(S_2P)$ that made him happy, etc. Wherever we have S, V, O, O, P, I, G, X, or Y, a nexus is either denoted or implied.

What, then, is the essential difference between junction and nexus? Instead of the latter term many scholars use the word *predication* and then define this as the linguistic expression of a judgment. But though this definition is found over and over again in works on logic and grammar, I think it should be avoided, as it is true of one kind of predication only, which, though it plays the greatest part in treatises on logic, is far from covering the majority of those sentences that occur in everyday conversations—and these should be the staple stock of linguistics. It would probably be best in linguistics to avoid the word predication altogether on account of its traditional connexion with logical theories. In grammar we should, not of course forget our logic, but steer clear of everything that may hamper our comprehension of language as it is actually used; this is why I have coined the new term nexus with its exclusive application to grammar. This has the additional advantage that nexus is applicable to a combination like *him happy* in *made him happy, thought him happy,* which cannot, perhaps, be called a predication and does not form a complete sentence.

33. 2. Junction and Nexus.

The difference between junction and nexus can, perhaps, be appreciated by means of my old comparison: a junction is like a picture, a nexus like a drama. Junction is agglutination, nexus is fusion. A junction describes, a nexus puts something in action, sets something going. Junction is static, nexus dynamic. Or we may say that in a junction we add one dead piece to another, as bricks are placed on top of and by the side of one another to build a house. But in a nexus we get life and movement. With a junction we are in the realm of mechanics, while a nexus belongs to biology. Junction is dead, nexus living; something happens in a nexus.[1]

But all this is figurative speech, and we get nearer the simple truth by saying that *a junction serves to make what we are talking about more definite or precise,* while *a nexus tells us something* by placing two (or more) definite ideas in relation to one another.

33. 3. Diagram.

The following diagram shows the relation of the various units that may be brought together in a nexus:

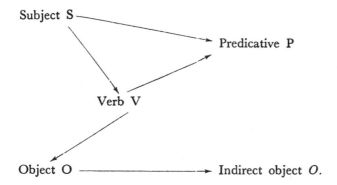

In the place of V we may have an Infinitive I, a Gerund G, a Nexus-substantive X, or an Agent-noun (or Participle) Y. Each of these can be connected with one or both of the upper-storey items, S and P, and likewise with one or both of the lower-storey items, O and *O*.

The scheme shows V as the central point: on this everybody has always agreed. The verb is the chief life-giving element in the most usual type of sentence. But it would be totally wrong to say that the existence of a finite verb was a *conditio sine qua non* of a normal sentence: in Ch. **9**.6 we have seen plenty of proofs to the contrary

---

[1] This is expressed in the German term *vorgang;* Meillet proposes to use *procès* as a grammatical term in French, but does not perhaps mean the same thing as I do by *nexus.*

in the so-called "nominal sentences" in which S and P together are quite sufficient to express a complete and independent thought. In a dependent nexus a V can even better be dispensed with, see Ch. **14** ff.

The life-giving power is found in the highest degree in the finite verb, which we therefore designate as V. It is found in a lesser degree in infinitives, gerunds, nexus-substantives and agent-nouns, and these four may be said to form a decreasing scale, in which the life-giving power is more and more diminished: an I has less of it than V, G less than I, X less than G, and Y least of all. But as this is so, it is a pity that when one asks an ordinary grammarian about a verb, he will invariably name the infinitive, *amare, lieben* etc., in English even with the particle *to*: *to love,* although *to* does not form a necessary appendix to the infinitive, still less to the verb as such.[1]

As will be seen from the arrows, there is a direct line of connexion between S and V as well as between S and P besides one from S through V to P; on the other hand there is a connexion from V to O and through O to *O* but no direct line from V to *O* nor from S or P to O or *O* : these are reached only through the medium of V or its substitutes.

In accordance with this the reader will in the preceding chapters have found many examples of the combinations S V, S P, S V P, V O, V O *O* (or V *O* O),[2] but none of S O or S *O* without an intervening verbal element, nor of P O or P *O*.

We shall now consider these things in greater detail.

33. 4. Rank in Nexus.

Leaving P out of account for the moment, we may say that S, O and *O* are the fixed points in an ordinary sentence, placed round V as the centre. If given a sentence like "John gave Mary a kiss" and asked "What is talked about here?" the man in the street will no doubt answer: "three things, John, Mary and the kiss", and the grammarian should agree with this common-sense answer. This is why I have always in previous publications taken these three, S, O, and *O,* as "primaries". I thus applied the theory of ranks to nexus as well as to junction, as I was struck with the similarity be-

---

[1] One may even see in an enumeration of auxiliary verbs *to shall* (e.g. Vendryes, Langage 99)—though *shall* never occurs in the infinitive!
[2] These generally preceded by S.

tween the two kinds of combinations, *(the) furiously barking dog,* which I designated as 3—2—1, and *(the)dog barked furiously,* which I therefore analyzed as primary—secondary—tertiary, 1—2—3. I found the same scale, though in reverse order, in both cases. *Dog* in both cases is the fixed, supreme point, to which the others are subordinated in a descending scale. It has been objected to this that the two combinations are not grammatically analogous, and that in thus parallelling *barks* and *barking* I overlook what is just the chief characteristic of the finite verb, its capacity of forming a complete sentence. My answer is that so far from overlooking this I have in my terminology provided names for a distinction between the two combinations by calling one a junction and the other a nexus ; one forming in general only one member of a sentence, while the other is capable of forming a complete sentence (though it does not always necessarily do so). But this difference in life-giving capacity does not exclude a similarity in inner structure, and just as everybody recognizes the analogy with regard to *furiously,* which is 3 in both combinations, I think I am right in placing *barking* and *barks* on the same level in the scale, between 1 *(dog)* and 3 *(furiously)*—though not otherwise identifying them. Compare also with a passive participle "he wounds him dangerously" and "a dangerously wounded warrior".

33. 5. Objection.

Western in his Norsk riksmålsgrammatikk followed my theory of ranks, but in a subsequent article (Mål og minne, 1934, p. 76) he says that the idea of rank can be applied to junctions only : a verb according to him falls outside the three ranks and forms a class by itself, the chief characteristic of which is that it may be determined by a tertiary. He is led to this conclusion by classing together the finite verb and the infinitive verb. It is true that both may be determined by a tertiary : he sings merrily, to sing merrily, this even when the infinitive is the subject, thus a primary. But Western overlooks the simple fact that an infinitive always denotes a nexus between a subject and the verbal idea, though the subject need not be expressly stated (see already in my first treatment of nexus, De to hovedarter, p. 35, PhilGr 141 ff., and below **34.**5). Therefore when we say that an infinitive is a primary (subject, or object), what we really mean is that the infinitival nexus, not the infinitive as such, is subject or object.

Now we understand why it is possible to have a tertiary in "to sing merrily is a pleasure" and "I want to sing merrily", for these sentences, if fully symbolized, are S(S⁰ I 3) V P and S V O(S⁰ I 3) : within each of the parentheses we have the three ranks 123, and the verbal element here as in "I sing merrily" is secondary. The same remark applies to English "(live and) let live", "let go", "make believe", F. "j'entends chanter dans la rue", Dan. "lad vaske ude", etc., in which there is no subject expressed with the infinitive. The relation between the elements is the same as in "I make him sing merrily" S V Oʳ(S₂ I 3).

When an infinitive is combined with a secondary, as in G. "Ein muntres singen, das muntre singen der studenten", the infinitive is really a nexus-substantive (as infinitives were admittedly from the origin), and the cases are parallel to E. "A merry life, the merry singing".

33. 6. Specializing.

If a subject and an object (direct or indirect) are termed primaries and thus compared with and coordinated with primaries in a junction, it is because they denote comparatively definite and special notions,[1] whereas the notion expressed by a verb is less "substantial" and therefore in comparison with S, O, *O* must be called secondary. But *the relation between primary and secondary is not the same in a nexus as in a junction.* There is this fundamental difference that while in a junction a secondary serves to make the primary more definite, more special, than it is in itself, this is not at all the case in a nexus. We may even with a certain degree of justification say that the notion expressed by a verb is made more definite by the subject : *goes* is specified in different ways when we say that the minister, the watch, time, a rumour goes, etc. It is even more true to say that an object "serves to make the meaning contained in the verb more special", PhilGr 158, where among other examples are found :

she sings well	she sings French songs
send for the doctor	send the boy for the doctor
he doesn't smoke	he doesn't smoke cigars.

This specializing power is especially evident with verbs of general

---

[1] On the indefinite S in sentences with *there is* see **34**.8.

import: he does harm, sums, his duty, wrong; he makes a noise, makes way, peace; F. il fait du bruit, etc.

An indirect object also specifies, compare thus "he offers a reward" and "he offers the butler a reward".

As a tertiary, too, has the effect of specializing or defining a verb (he walks fast, sings loud, etc.) we understand how it is that the boundary between object and tertiary is often fluctuating: above (**7**.4) we saw instances of O/3 or 3/O, see also below **36**.4.

If the specifying power of the different ranks were not in this way the reverse in a nexus of what it is in a junction, we should not easily understand the shiftings found especially with nexus-substantives, where *the doctor* (primary) *arrives* (sec.) becomes *the doctor's* (sec.) *arrival* (primary); cf. **39**.4.

Though the terms primary and secondary are thus applicable to the parts of a nexus, there is no need to mark this by means of numerals as the big initials are sufficient to show the relation.

CHAPTER 34.

Subject.

34. 1. Definition.

What is a subject? How to define it? That the grammatical subject cannot be sufficiently defined as "that about which we speak" has already been mentioned (**33**.4). This was seen very clearly many years ago by H. G. Wiwel (Synspunkter for dansk sproglære. 1901) and has been stated, independently, by P. B. Ballard (Thought and Language. 1934, p. 90) in a passage which I transcribe: "The subject of a sentence ... is supposed to state what the speaker is going to speak about. How is the supposition realised in the following sentence: *I saw in the city yesterday a big fire blazing away with flames thirty feet high?* What am I talking about here? Grammar says it is myself; common sense says it is a fire in the city. What arrests my attention is not the explicit predication *I saw,* but the predication lying latent in the phrase *a big fire blazing away.* The predications are here topsy-turvy. What is grammatically important is logically unimportant; for *I saw* is lugged in as a mere excuse for making an extraordinary statement, and is intended to be kept in the background."

In MEG III 11.1$_5$ I said: "the [grammatical] subject cannot be defined by means of such words as active or agent; this is excluded by the meaning of a great many verbs, e.g. *suffer* ... The subject is the primary which is most intimately connected with the verb (predicate) in the form which it actually has in the sentence with which we are concerned; thus *Tom* is the subject in (1) "Tom beats John", but not in (2) "John is beaten by Tom", though both sentences indicate the same action on the part of Tom; in the latter sentence *John* is the subject, because he is the person most intimately connected with the verb *beat* in the actual form employed: *is beaten.* We can thus find out the subject by asking *Who* (or *What*) followed by the verb in the form used in the sentence: (1) Who beats (John)? Tom / (2) Who is beaten (by Tom)? John.—Subject as a grammatical term can thus be defined only in connexion with the rest of the sentence in its actual form. From such sentences in the most typical form the term is transferred to other forms of nexus (SP; SG; SI; SX) and even to the use in "Out with you!" 3 pSI **(13.1)** and analogous cases.

34. 2. **Case.**

The case used to express the subject is generally the nominative, in dependent nexuses it may be the accusative. In some cases Russian has the genitive in negative sentences; Finnish has the partitive if the subject is indefinite. In a dependent tertiary (above **14**.5) S is in the ablative in Latin, in the genitive in Greek, in the dative in Gothic or Slavic, in the accusative in German, in the nominative in English and Spanish (PhilGr 126—129); the same case is used in the P of such constructions. The S of a gerund may, and the S of a nexus-substantive generally must be in the genitive.

The constructions dealt with in **14**.5 are not well named in traditional grammar. In my school-days we spoke of "duo ablativi" in Latin (but the number is not decisive, and in other languages other cases than the ablative are used) or "ablativi consequentiae" (which says nothing); a frequent name is "absolute construction" (ablative absolute); "absolute participle" is also said (but a participle need not enter into the construction); *absolute* here means 'having no connexion with the rest of the sentence', but this negative definition really explains nothing. I analyze the construction as a nexus (SP) standing in the sentence as tertiary, thus 3(SP), and consequently use the term "nexus tertiary", which says everything necessary in a simple way, provided my terms nexus and tertiary (which are so useful in many ways) are once accepted.

34. 3. No Subject.

We have verbal sentences without a subject; but these are of different kinds. In the first place we have examples like L. *cantat,* It. and other Romanic languages *canta,* where English has *he* (or *she*) *sings*; who it is that sings appears from the context, whether a name has just been mentioned in the preceding sentence or is clear from the situation only. The form of the verb shows nothing else beside the *negative* fact that the singer is neither identical with the speaker nor with the person or persons spoken to. This is supposed to be a direct continuation of the original Indo-European practice, in which the finite verb was self-containing (autonomous), i.e. was sufficient in itself to fill out a whole sentence, a whole communication. If there was a subject this stood in "extraposition", outside the sentence proper; the same is true of an object. The later development led to the subject (and object) coming into closer and closer connexion with the verb—in practically the same way in which what was originally an adverb and an independent noun came to be a preposition and a case governed by a preposition. Survivals of this old practice, *canta,* etc., should be denoted S^0 V; they are not essentially different from such English instances as *sings* in "(He comes here every evening and) sings". Other English examples of the same type S^0 V are found in idiomatic phrases like "Thank you!" or "Confound it!"

In a second type of sentence the form of the verb gives *positive* information of the subject: L., It., Sp. *canto,* L., Sp. *cantas,* It. *canti,* etc. For this we have the symbol with the two letters bracketed $\left\{ SV \right\}$.

Bracketing must also be used for those forms of the imperative which show the person indubitably, L. *canta,* G. *sing,* Dan. *syng,* and in the first person pl. L. *cantemus,* Sp. *cantemos* (Subjunctive), It. *cantiamo,* F. *chantons,* all of them are $\left\{ SV \right\}$. The same symbolization may be used also for imperatives whose forms are not to the same extent unambiguous, e.g. E. *sing,* F. *chante.* Here, however, the symbol S^0 V may be used.

34. 4. Pluit.

While in the cases so far considered there can be no doubt what
would be the subject if it were expressed, this is not the case in the
sentences with which we are now going to deal. First the so-called
impersonal verbs to express natural phenomena: L. *pluit*, It. *piove*,
Sp. *llove*. Here the other West-European languages now add a
(definite!) pronoun as S: *it rains, es regnet, det regner, il pleut*:
unspecified neuter, "das grosse neutrum der natur" (see PhilGr 241).
It would, I think, be wrong in the symbolization too explicitly to
follow this modern feeling, as we should, were we to write *pluit*
S^0 V: much better recognize that there are one-member sentences
and write simply V (Cf. PhilGr 307 and Amorphous sentences above
26).[1] Nor should I use S^0 in symbolizing such sentences as G.
Hier ist kalt ; Dan. *Her er koldt* 3 V P, or the Dan. passive *Her rulles*
('Mangling done here') 3 V^b.

34. 5. Infinitives, etc.

An infinitive, a gerund, and a nexus-substantive all of them
presuppose a nexus, i.e. a combination of the verbal element with a
subject. In many cases both are expressed, thus in *I want him to sing*
S V $O(S_2I)$, *I admire his singing* S V $O(S^2{}_2G)$, *I admire his per-
formance* S V $O(S^2{}_2X)$.

But extremely often the subject is left to be inferred from the
context. It may be identical with the subject of the main verb:
I want to sing S V $O(S^0I)$; *He is afraid of dying* S W $O(S^0G)$;
or some other part of the sentence: *It bores her to sing* s V O S
$(IS^0{}_2 = O)$; *it is her delight to sing* s V $P(1^{*2}1)S(IS^{*0})$.

In many combinations the latent subject of an infinitive, gerund,
or nexus-substantive is the 'generic person' = F. *on*, which in this
paragraph is indicated by the symbol S^∞ :
To see is to believe $S(IS^{0\,\infty})$ V $P(I_2S^{0\,\infty})$.
Seeing is believing $S(GS^{0\,\infty})$ V $P(G_2S^{0\,\infty})$.
Activity produces happiness $S(XS_2{}^{0\,\infty})$ V $O^r(X_2S_2{}^{0\,\infty})$.

---

[1] It was easy enough to reduce *pluit* to the ordinary type of two-member
sentence so long as the *-t* was considered the remnant of an original subject-
pronoun ; but this conception can no longer be maintained.—It is interesting
to note the use without the otherwise necessary *es, il* in infinitives like "Lass
regnen, wenn es regnen will" and "Quand il pleut, nous laissons pleuvoir"
(But "when it rains we let it rain", Dan. "når det regner, lar vi det
regne").—In Magyar one finds "esik az eső" 'the rain rains', cp. Shakespeare's "But the rain it raineth every day".

In ordinary symbolization such indication of $S^{0\,\infty}$ seems superfluous.

Now and then the latent subject may be different according as an infinitive or a gerund is chosen:

He likes to sing S V O(S^0I).

He likes singing S V O($S_2^{0\,\infty}$ G),

but usage is not uniform on this point.

In ch. **13**.1 "Let us go" is analyzed V O(SI)!, while later the apparently identical sentence is written $\{SV\}$ O O(I)! The former (which may be pronounced *let's go*) corresponds to F *allons-nous-en*, the latter to *permettez-nous d'aller*. In the former, but not in the latter, we have the 'inclusive' plural of $I = $ 'I and you'.

34. 6. The Weak There.

This word presents various grammatical peculiarities.[1] It is evident that it originated as the ordinary *there*, a "pronominal adverb" meaning "at that particular place", but in course of time it has diverged very considerably from its origin, not only in pronunciation, where it has the weak indistinct [ə]-sound instead of the diphthong [ɛ·ə], but in other respects as well. The semantic weakening is seen especially where the same sentence contains both *there*'s: "There were many people there". Among grammatical peculiarities it suffices here to mention the use with an infinitive and a gerund: "Let there be light | You wouldn't like there to be a revolution | It is necessary for there to be a change | On account of there being no taxis.

Some, but not all, of these peculiarities are found also with the corresponding adverbs Dan. *der*, and Du. *er*.

In some respects (place in the sentence, etc.) this *there* behaves as an ordinary subject, and many grammarians therefore class it as a kind of subject, and call it "formal subject", "makeshift subject" (Wiwel, Synsp. f. dansk sprogl.: "nødsubjekt"), "sham subject" (Western, Norsk riksmålsgr. "skinsubjekt"), "preparatory" or "anticipatory subject". These last-mentioned names are not pertinent,

---

[1] See my own Spr. log. 1913 (where earlier literature is quoted), PhilGr 154 ff., R. Ljunggren, Om den opersonliga konstruktionen 1926, Aage Hansen, Sætningen og dens led, 1933, 49 ff., E. Oxenvad in Studier tilegnede V. Dahlerup, 1934.

for *there* need not come first, see, e.g. "I don't know what there can be said in his favour | Shoes there were none | What other explanation was there? | The reason, if reason there was ... | One gate there only was (Milton) | Dan. Een udvej var der dog,—and other instances in which for the sake of emphasis or for grammatical reasons the "real subject" is placed before *there*. The best name would probably be "existential *there*", as it generally indicates (vaguely) the existence of something on which fuller information is to follow. As a non-committal symbol I have chosen 3/s, which indicates the alternative analysis, tertiary or "lesser subject". It is not absolutely necessary that the sentence contains a "subject" though this seems to be the invariable rule in English: in Danish we have such passive constructions as *der danses* 'there is dancing', cp. the G. *es* in *es wird getanzt*.

34. 7. Introductory there.

Still, apart from such cases and from the above-mentioned cases in which the subject precedes *there,* we may say that the general rule is to use *there* as an introduction, after which we have a verb and then a subject. It would not be absolutely wrong to look upon *there* (Dan. *der*) as a device to bring about the word-order verb—subject. In comparing the Authorized Version with the Greek original I was struck with the frequency of this *there* before a verb, where the original had a verb first, before the subject.

Then we may ask, Why is this word-order preferred in such cases in languages which ordinarily place the subject before the verb? The reason is to be sought, partly in the nature of the verb, partly in that of the subject. The verb is most often one of vague meaning, expressing mere existence (*is, exists*) or such forms of existence as *stand, lie, come,* etc., while the construction is not usual with verbs of more definite meaning: instead of "there took a man his hat" we prefer saying "there was a man who took his hat".[1]

34. 8. Subject Indefinite.

The subject, too, presents some peculiarities in such "existential sentences". It is not possible in them to have a generic subject (com-

---

[1] The rule is not carried through with the same consistency in English as in Danish: I have several quotations from Chaucer up to recent writers of *there* + transitive verb + object.

prising a whole species), because it is too definite. "Whether or not a word like *there* is used to introduce [existential sentences], the verb precedes the subject, and the latter is hardly treated grammatically like a real subject". (PhilGr 155 with remarks on Dan. *dem* after *der er*, etc.) Oxenvad goes one step further than I do; he will not recognize it as a subject: "though it carries out (er udøver af) the verbal idea, it is subordinate to the verb", thus what he calls a "side-led" (side-member)—this word is used by Dan. grammarians as a comprehensive term for O, O and P. I had stressed the general definiteness of the subject in ordinary sentences as contrasted to these, Oxenvad even goes so far as to say: "An indefinite subject is an absurdity (en meningsløshed)".

The tendency to indefiniteness is shown in the demonstrative pronoun; this in other sentences is definite enough, but in the combination "there are those who think", Dan. "der er dem som mener" it has the same indefinite meaning as *some*; similarly the neuter singular "there was that in his behaviour which ...", "der var det som ...". A difference from the ordinary subjects further appears in the possible use of *that*, Dan. *det* in cases like: "Are there advantages in this scheme? Yes, *that* there are (or, Yes, there are *that*)", Dan. "er der fordele ved den plan? Ja, *det* er der": the neutral singular *that, det* is used, as if we had to deal with a predicative, not a subject.

34. 9. Analogous Expressions.

In PhilGr 155—156 mention is made of various ways in which languages which have nothing directly corresponding to this *there* express the same sort of existence, always with the "subject" after the verb, and often in such a way that formally it is an object, thus after F. *il y a*, Sp. *hay*, G. *es gibt* (where dialects have *es geben* before a plural word). In Ch. **8**.8 some examples of this kind are collected and symbolized O/S, because one may hesitate whether to call them objects or subjects, or should we say that they are neither?

CHAPTER 35.

Subject and Predicative.

35. 1. S is P.

While the relation between subject and predicative is simple enough where they are immediately connected (SP or PS), whether this combination is independent, forming a sentence (see **9**.6),[1] or dependent as forming part of a sentence (see **14**), it is somewhat more complicated where their connexion is mediated through a verb: S V P as in *Tom is happy, looks happy, became president,* etc. Logicians will try to make us believe that all sentences (or all "judgments") can be reduced, or for the sake of logical inferences should be reduced, to the type "S is P", but though they are followed in this by some well-known students of language who even call this the "urform" of sentences, it should really be beneath the dignity of serious grammarians to use all kinds of tricks in order to press the infinite variety of living language into this strait-jacket. But though not universal, this type is important, and we must ask: how is this S V P to be understood?

35. 2. Hammerich.

An interesting interpretation is given by L. L. Hammerich.[2] He uses the symbols S subject, P predicate (which should not be confounded with my own P = predicative), s partial subject, p partial predicate. This denotation, perhaps, is not very practical as the shapes of big (capital) S and P and small s and p as presented in his diagrams are not always easily distinguishable. To avoid misunderstanding I add everywhere the adjective big and small in the following exposition of Hammerich's views.

A sentence like *the horse is ill* is dissolved into two predications, one consisting of *the horse* (small s)—*ill* (small p), and the other consisting of this first predication *the horse ill* as forming together the subject (big S) of *is* (big P), *is* being taken in the sense 'exists': "Also wo das deutsche (wie das lateinische u. s. w.) *das pferd ist*

---

[1] Where in our modern languages we have PS as an independent sentence, it is often formed in this way that P is said by itself, as if it might stand alone, and S is added as an afterthought.

[2] In A Grammatical Miscellany offered to Otto Jespersen. 1930, p. 305 ff., Actes du Deuxième Congrès de Linguistes, Genève 1933, p. 195 ff., Indledning til tysk grammatik. 1935, p. 40 ff.

krank sagt, haben diese sprachen einen ausdruck, dessen sinn so ist: *pferd krank*—(das ist) *wirklichkeit.* Das ist aber so ziemlich dasselbe als das, was als grundbedeutung des ausdruckes *das pferd ist krank, eqvus aegrotus est* erschlossen wurde."

Similarly *das pferd wird krank = krankheit des pferdes tritt ein; das pferd bleibt krank = krankheit des pferdes setzt das dasein fort, besteht andauernd,* etc.

We may represent his view in this way:

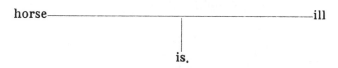

But—even apart from the, to me, doubtful idea that nominal expressions (with nexus-substantives) are supposed to be more primitive than verbs—the whole thing seems to me unnatural. To the modern feeling, at any rate, *is* in such sentences does not mean 'exists' (and when philosophers form sentences like "God is", this is felt as a rather unnatural transference from the normal use of *is* as "copula"). The man in the street would feel much more at home in such a figure as this:

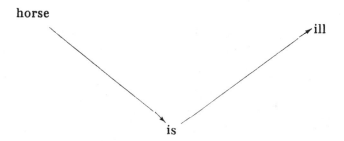

If we answer the question: "Is he dead?" by saying: "Yes, he is"—does that mean: "he exists" or "his death exists"?

With other verbs the interpretation is even more unnatural: Hammerich himself says that in *er heisst Christian* the meaning of *heisst* is 'existiert als benennung'. Now, what would a similar paraphrase be like if applied to such sentences as *the natives go naked | she stood godmother to his little boy,* or even *he went mad | il tomba malade?* It seems much better to face the facts squarely and say that (just as in *John beats Tom* S V O) we have in S V P a nexus consisting of three elements in one particular grammatical "figure", and then to add that "some verbs when connected with predicatives tend to lose their full meaning and approach the function of an empty link" (MEG III 17.1).

Hammerich is obliged from his analysis to say that in *die pferde sind krank* it is really illogical to have the plural form of the verb, for the logical subject of the verb is not *die pferde,* but the nexus *pferde krank = krankheit der pferde : krankheit der pferde ist.*

Nor can I see that *der sohn wurde Johannes getauft* should be logically analyzed *der sohn* (small s) *Johannes* (small p)—both together (big S) *wurde getauft* (big P). He even says himself : „Aber das sprachbewusstsein fasst den zusammenhang sicher anders auf, nämlich als der sohn (big S) wurde Johannes getauft (all this big P)." Quite so, if we accept the usual definition of predicate as everything in a sentence that is not the subject. (But *Johannes* is P^r to *wurde getauft*).

Hammerich's analysis of still another German sentence deserves quotation (but I do not like the words *ursprünglich* and *urteile*) : "*Der flieger wurde verloren geglaubt* enthält ursprünglich drei urteile : I der flieger : s^1—verloren : p^1, II (der flieger—verloren) : s^2 —geglaubt : p^2, III (der flieger—verloren—geglaubt) : s^3—wurde : p^3 ; die verbindung der prädikatselemente ergibt : der flieger : S— wurde verloren geglaubt : P".

Instead of this I should say : This sentence is the passive of *man glaubte den flieger verloren;* I analyze the active S V O(S$_2$P), and in accordance with **16**.1 above I symbolize the passive : $\frac{1}{2}$S V^b $\frac{1}{2}$S(P), in which, of course, the passive V^b *wurde geglaubt* may ultimately be transcribed V P(Y^b).

Hammerich's manner of viewing these sentences is in some respects similar to—and may have been partly inspired by—my own analysis of sentences like "he happened to fall | he was sure to fall", etc. (MEG III 11.9, above Ch. **16**), but seems to me an example of a tenable idea carried too far and therefore leading to unjustified consequences. His theory is especially open to objection, I think, when he is implying that his logical analysis represents the origin of sentences containing a verb and a predicative. In most of these I fancy that the verb was originally used in its full sense, requiring no supplement in the form of a predicative, and that some subsidiary complement was added occasionally in the form of an extraposition : later this could be more and more incorporated into the sentence itself and by that means felt to be directly connected with the verb (MEG III 17.1 ff.). Sentences containing *is* probably have their origin in a different way, namely from "nominal sentences" in which two words were formlessly placed together as subject and predicative; later these were brought under the usual type by the addition of the least substantial verb (paradoxically termed verbum substantivum), in much the same way as other sentences were made to conform to the usual type by the addition of the colourless subject *it* (it rains, it pleases me to go, etc.). But questions of supposed original development should not determine our analysis of things as they are in our own day.

35. 3. Rank of Predicative.

With regard to the predicative (P) the question of rank is not quite so simple as in the case of S, O, and O. P seems to be a primary in "Shakespeare is the author of Hamlet", but it seems equally certain that in "this rose is red" the predicative *red* is a secondary, just as in "a red rose". In most of the languages which inflect adjectives in number and gender, the predicative adjective agrees in these two respects with the subject, just as they agree with the primary in a junction. It should, however, be noted that where a distinction is made between an adjectival and a substantival form in the possessive pronouns, the latter is used as a P: this is mine (not *my*), c'est le mien (not *mon*).

Some would even go further and say that a predicative can be not only a primary and a secondary, according to circumstances, but even a tertiary, as in John is *here,* or the war is *over.* Or should we call *over* a secondary here?

In nearly all cases in which a subject and a predicative are connected by means of *is,* the meaning is not to assert complete identity, but rather that the subject belongs to, i.e. forms part of, the class denoted by the predicative.

In some idiomatic expressions we have only seemingly complete identity. This is well expressed by Sigwart (Logic, as quoted by Keynes, Studies in Formal Logic, 52) : "In the proposition, *Children are children,* the subject-term means only the age characteristic of childhood; the predicate-term the other characteristics which are connected with it."

In PhilGr p. 151 ff. I speak of the logical relation between subject and predicative and say that if one of the two words connected by *is* is more special than the other, it becomes by that fact alone subject. This has been challenged by some writers, but I think my thesis is perfectly defensible. No one has disputed my thesis with regard to the examples "Tom is a scoundrel, the thief was a coward, a cat is a mammal", nor my explanation that in "My brother was captain of the vessel" *my brother* is the more special term (meaning 'my only brother', or 'the brother of whom we were just talking'— It. *il mio fratello*) and therefore the subject; while in "The captain of the vessel was my brother" *my brother* is less definite (it means It. *un mio fratello* 'one of my brothers', or leaves the question open whether I have more than one), and therefore it here is the predicative.

In the System of Grammar p. 23 (= Linguistica 322) I dealt with some objections propounded by Brøndal and showed that even such a sentence as "All is vanity", rightly interpreted, confirms rather than confutes my thesis, as it means that whatever special and definite thing you may take falls under the more comprehensive (and accordingly indefinite) class of what the Preacher calls vanity. That this was a paradox was evidently not hidden to him, or he would not have said it.

"Where there is perfect identity (coextension) of the two terms connected by *is,* they may change places as subject and predicative; this [i.e. perfect identity] is what Keats implied in his line: "Beauty is truth; truth, beauty"." This passage (found in PhilGr p. 153) elicited the following exclamation from Gardiner (Speech and Language p. 287) : "Is he (Jespersen) maintaining that Keats was wishing to bring home to his audience a purely grammatical fact? Surely this is to do monstrous injustice to the poet", etc. Is not Gardiner here doing monstrous injustice to a poor grammarian, who may be allowed sometimes to extract grammatical as well as poetic honey from one and the same line? Surely I did not dream for a moment in penning the above passage that my remark could be interpreted otherwise than as indicated in the words here inserted in square brackets.

Anyhow Gardiner is curiously wrong when he asserts that "Jespersen's criterion fails altogether when, in a sentence with the copula, subject and predicate are coextensive". On the contrary it is confirmed in the most indubitable way. For if extension is made a criterion, and if there are cases in which the extension is equal, this means that we cannot decide which is subject and which predicative.

Take the sentence "The only man who knew the secret was Tom"
—this may be symbolized either
S(212(S^c V O)) V P, or
P(212(S^c V O)) V S.

As this means the same thing as "Tom was the only man who knew the secret", we may write S/P V P/S.

The special circumstances regarding the rank of a predicative are the reason why in the diagram in **33**.3 P was placed in a line by itself, lower than S.

In Arabic grammar we meet with interesting things illustrating the role of definiteness (I know them only from Steinthal, Charakteristik d. typen des sprachbaues 264 f.). In a junction the adjective agrees with the subst. not only in gender, number and case, but also in definite or indefinite form. If the sb. is definite, but the adj. indefinite, the latter is P, not adjunct, but no copula is used; if P is definite like the substantive, *huwa* is inserted as copula. An indefinite subject is rare, except "wenn das prädikat aus einem adverbialen bestimmung besteht: In der-moschee (ist) ein esel"—corresponding to our sentences with *there is*.

35. 4. Case of Predicative.

The ordinary case of the predicative is the nominative on account of its close connexion with the subject. Russian uses the instrumental in speaking of a transitory state. Finnish has (alongside of the nominative) the two cases essive for permanent states and translative for what here is written P^r. On the case in a dependent nexus see **34**.2.

CHAPTER 36.

Object.

36. 1. Ordinary Objects.

Next we go on to consider the lower storey of the diagram in **33**.2. There we find the object, which is less intimately connected with the verb (in the actual form this has in the sentence concerned) than either the subject or the predicative; if there are two objects the direct object O is more intimately connected with the verb than the indirect object *O*. What is the object of a verbal sentence is found (see MEG III 12.1) by asking *Whom*, or *What* with the subject and verb of the sentence. Among the various kinds of objects it is easy to single out objects of result O^r, but apart from them we find the most heterogeneous relations between verb and object, as transitive verbs cover an enormous portion of all the multifarious activities and happenings found in human life. To speak of a "causal connexion" between verb and object really leads to nothing, apart from the object of result.

36. 2. Complex Verbal Expressions.

An O may stand not only after a simple verb (including such composite expressions as *has taken, is taking, will take, can take,* etc.), but also after a complex verbal phrase consisting of a verb and one or more words which together with the verb form one notion; this is denoted by the symbol W (examples see **8**.5). Note the difference between (a) *she put on her things,* in which *her things* is simply the object of *put,* and *on* is an adverb (tertiary), which may in certain cases be placed after the object: *she put them on*— and on the other hand (b) *she waited on us,* where *on* is a preposition with *us* at its regimen and is always placed before it. While *she put on her things* must be symbolized S V 3 O, *she waited on us* must be written S V p1, or better, considering *wait on* as a complex verbal phrase and *us* as the object of this: S W O. The justification of such symbolization is found in the fact that the verb together with what follows forms one *semantic* unit.[1] This, then, is the distinctive trait of W as against the above-mentioned combinations *has taken, can take,* etc., which form grammatical rather than semantic units.

Other verbal complexes with their equivalents:
Look at something = consider, regard.
Think of something = consider.
Walk with someone = accompany.
Be afraid of something = fear.
Laugh at = mock, deride.
Speak of = mention.

---

[1] Cf. R. Körner, Objektet, in Moderna språk, 1935, p. 58 ff. On p. 64 the author calls attention to the difference in the use of the simple pronoun and the *self*-pronoun between *he looked in front of him* S V pp1 (S) and *he looked at himself in the glass* S W O(S) p1.

Get rid of = discard, pack off.

Shake hands with = greet.

Make much of = esteem.

Find fault with = criticize, rebuke, etc. But the use of the symbol W
    is not restricted to cases in which we have one-word equivalents.

See also the lists in MEG III 10.2_2 ff. and note the difference
between instances in which it is possible and others in which it is
impossible to place the preposition last in a relative clause, ib 10.3_5.

36. 3. Doubtful Cases.

Perhaps in the first part of this work some readers wonder at the
extensive use I have made of the symbol O, e.g. when I denote the
infinitive in *he has to go* as the object of the verb *has*. I think it may
be justified when we consider that the sentence means the same thing
as "he has the task to go", where *the task* is evidently the object of
has. To my mind there is no doubt that the object in "we thought
him guilty; we saw him run" is not simply *him,* but the whole nexus
him guilty and *him run;* the logical consequence of this is the introduction of the symbol $\frac{1}{2}$S and $\frac{1}{2}$O, examples of which are seen
in Ch. **16**. But it must be admitted that there are doubtful cases
and that the application of the symbol O is not always easy.

Infinitives and clauses are sometimes placed without a preposition,
where a preposition would be required before a substantive. A notation with p^0 would be cumbrous. I should use the symbol O in cases
like the following:

His plan to go to France $S^2XO(I\ p1)$; cf. he planned to ...

My belief that he will come $S^2XO(3^cS_2V)$.

The idea that he will come $1O(3^cS\ V)$.

I shall be careful what I do S V P $O(O_2SV)$.

I shall be careful not to say this S V P $O(3^nIO_2)$.

He insisted that she must come S V $O(3^cS_2V)$.

I shall see you are no loser S V $O(S_2VP(2Y))$.

I am of opinion this is the best course S W $O(S_2VP(21))$.

That reminds me what a fool he was S V O $O_2(P(2!1)\ S_2\ V)$.

He was at a loss what to say S W $O(O_2?I)$.

A gentleman anxious to avoid a scandal $12(YO(IO_2))$—Y doubtful.

His pretensions to be infallible S^2 X $O(IP)$.

I wonder who is ill S V $O(S_2?\ VP)$.

But in some, at any rate, of these the difficulty may be evaded
by the use of the symbol for apposition and extraposition [ ].

36. 4. Case of Object.

The ordinary case of the object is the accusative in most of those Indo-European languages that keep up the old case distinctions. This rule, however, is not universal. We have the genitive in Slavic languages, not only if the sentence is negative, but also in other cases. The dative is used pretty extensively, e.g. in German after *helfen, schaden* and other well-known verbs, in Latin after *nocere, obedire,* etc. After some verbs, where we take the following substantive as an ordinary object, other languages think of it as the instrument, thus Ru. *brosat' kamen'jami* (instrumental), 'throw stones', and correspondingly Icelandic *kasta steinum* (dative) : we might write V 3/O, though there is no objection to the simple V O.

36. 5. Indirect Object.

In the symbols here used two kinds of objects are recognized, direct O and indirect *O*. The distinction involves some rather knotty problems, especially when we leave the field of English, where everything is comparatively simple and easy.

As explained in MEG III 14.1, the direct object is more intimately connected with the verb than the indirect object, in spite of the latter's seemingly privileged position in the great majority of the cases in which it is placed between V and O. In "they offered the man a reward" it is possible to isolate the direct object (*they offered a reward*), but not the indirect object (*they offered the man*). *A reward* is the object of *offered,* but *the man* is the object of *offered a reward.* It is, therefore, quite natural to ask "What did they offer?" but not "Whom (or To whom) did they offer?" without mentioning the object. Thus also in the passive : we can say, "A reward was offered", but not "The man was offered" without saying what; nor can we ask "Who was offered?" though it is possible to ask "Who was offered a reward?" as well as "What was offered?" Hence we may say that in "a reward was offered the man" *a reward* is the subject of *was offered,* but in the equally possible way of putting it "the man was offered a reward" *the man* is subject, not of *was offered,* but of the whole combination *was offered a reward.*

This relation is clearly indicated in the diagram in **33**.3.

The relation between direct and indirect objects bears a certain resemblance to that between the subject and the predicative; we might even say that O : O = S : P.

In the sentence "This will last me quite a long time" the correct symbol will be S V *O* O(321), because it is impossible to say "this will last me". Accordingly "this will last me till Christmas" is S V *O* O(p1), *till Christmas* being taken in the same way as the prepositional groups in **7**.5.

36. 6. Two Direct Objects.

When we have two objects with the same verb, it is sometimes doubtful whether they should be called O and *O* or O and O_2 (two direct objects). In MEG III 14.9 I have given reasons for the latter view in cases like

He struck him a heavy blow S V O O_2(21).

I envy you your money S V O $O_2(1^21)$.

because it is possible to say both *strike him* and *strike a blow*, both *envy you* and *envy your money*, and the verbs thus fall outside the criterion used in "offer him a reward", etc. But I expressly said that such combinations resemble those with *O* and O, and I should not feel at all surprised if some readers prefer these symbols; in the first sentence we might even think of writing *blow* as 3 or O/3.

In spite of some doubt I should transcribe

Dan. "Jeg erindrer mig dagen", as S V *O*(=S) O, with *mig* as *O*, because the usual phrase is "Jeg erindrer dagen" S V O; but

G. „Ich erinnere mich des tages" is perhaps rather S V O(S) O_2 with two "direct objects", cf. F. Je me souviens du jour S O(S) V pO_2 with the further consequence that "Je m'en souviens" is transcribed S O(S) O_2 V. It is, however, also possible to transcribe the German sentence S V *O*(S) O,

as it is one of the most important principles of our symbolization to take into consideration solely notional relations without regard to the actual forms in which these happen to be clothed in each language. But it must be admitted that as soon as we leave English it is often extremely difficult to tell what is the notional relation of two existing objects.

36. 7. *O* without O.

Is it possible to have an indirect object without a direct one? In cases like

I'll write you when I get to London;

F. Je lui pardonne—I transcribe S V *O* (F. S *O* V), because a

complete analysis must be S V *O* O⁰ (in the French instance
S *O* V O⁰) with a latent direct object, this O⁰ being in one case
something like "a letter", in the other "ses fautes, ce qu'il a commis",
or whatever it may be.

I do not think we should apply the same reasoning to G. *Ich
danke dir,* for though it is possible to say "Dir danke ich mein
ganzes glück" (quoted by Sonnenschein), which is *O* V S O, this
construction is rare except when *danke* means 'owe to you'; in the
ordinary everyday meaning one says "ich danke dir für den brief",
which according to our principles must be written S V O p1. Anyhow E. "I thank you", and Dan. "Jeg takker dig" must be symbolized S V O with direct object, as also F. "Je remercie ta mère de
sa bonté", etc. As already said, in spite of the dative we write O,
not *O,* after L. *noceo,* F. *nuire, obéir,* G. *schaden,* etc. In corrobora-
tion of this view we may recall the well-known fact that in the passive French has "vous serez obéi". (Similarly in Icelandic *ero þeir
þá holpnir* 'they were then helped' though *hjalpa* takes the dative).

I should even use the sign for direct object in "He looked
(stared) me in the face" S V O p1, because there is only one
object. But it may be said that *look (stare) in the face* is really W
though not standing together; we might also write S V* O p1*.

36. 8. F. à, E. to.

In French we have the well-known dative forms of the personal
pronouns, and there can be no doubt of applying the symbol *O* for
them in such cases as *Je lui donne (promets,* etc.) *un franc* S *O* V O.
But apart from these pronouns a combination with the preposition
à is used. Now I think it will be admitted that if I am right in using
the symbol pP—a predicative after a preposition—as above **9**.5 : she
grows into a tall girl S V pP(21), I am also justified in transcribing
Je donne un franc au garçon S V O p*O*.

This use of *à* is clearly distinct from that in Je vais au ministre
S V p1—where it is not possible to say *Je lui vais.*

A further consequence is that we transcribe

I give a shilling to the waiter; Dan. Jeg giver en krone til opvar-
     teren S V O p*O*.

But it must be said very emphatically that this is not the same
thing as recognizing *to the waiter* as a dative case.

It may even be possible that some scholars would use the same
symbols with other prepositions than *to:*

The University conferred a degree on Mr. N. S V O pO.
They bestowed a favour on him S V O pO.
He is setting a trap for you S V O pO.

But it will always be difficult to draw the line between this pO and an ordinary p1.

36. 9. Sp., Pg. a.

Special mention must here be made of the use of the preposition *á* (*a*) in Spanish and Portuguese (cf. *pe* in Rumanian) before the direct object. This is chiefly used with the name of a person (sometimes also an animal) and may be said to be a means of distinguishing between animate and inanimate (on similar distinctions in other languages see PhilGr 238) : *He visto Madrid,* but *he visto al ministro.* As the word-order S V O is not carried through, the preposition sometimes shows which is S and which O : *mató el perro al lobo* 'the dog killed the wolf', *mató al perro el lobo* 'the wolf killed the dog'. In *envió el hijo al padre* 'he sent the son to the father' *á* serves to distinguish O from *O*. This, however, is not carried through : I find (Galdós, Doña Perfecta 81) *Tengo el gusto de presentar á usted á mi querido Jacitillo,* where the first probably is the indirect object.[1]

In our symbols this combination of *á* and its regimen must be denoted pO and p*O* respectively.[2]

It will be seen that the name object and the symbols O and *O* are used here in various places for what is governed by a preposition (thus pO and p*O*), if the notional relation is the same that would (with other verbs) be expressed by a simple O or *O*.

---

[1] There are some interesting remarks on this *a* in the periodical Language 8.263 by H. V. Velten. Cf. also W. Havers, Handb. d. erklärenden syntax p. 201.

[2] One even finds a predicative with á : lo primero que vieron sus ojos fué a su doncella Rufina | el único disputado que conozco es a don Salustio (Valdés, Sinf. past. 12,147) : but it is true that this is conceived as O of *vieron* and *conozco*.

CHAPTER 37.

Passive.

37. 1. Symbols.

The symbolization is simple enough where there is a single verbal form, as in L. *amatur* and in the Scandinavian forms in *-s: elskes,* etc.: V^b. (That the latter forms were originally reflexive, from an added *sik,* has no importance for our purpose). But in the Romanic languages, in English, German and Dutch, the passive is formed by means of auxiliaries, and the same is the case in the Scandinavian periphrases with *bliver (blir)* and *er.* Here the full symbolization would be S V P(Y^b) for He was loved; F. il était aimé; G. er war (wurde) geliebt; Dan. han var (blev) elsket—and S V P^r(Y^b) for He was killed; F. Il fut tué; G. Er wurde getötet; Dan. Han blev dræbt, etc.

Above, however, all such passives have been written uniformly S V^b, which must be considered a practical, but harmless simplification, similar in character to that which makes us write *has killed, will kill,* etc., simply as V.

No further comment is surely necessary to explain the examples quoted in **8**.7: the occurrence of O, *O* and the prepositional indication within parentheses of what in the active was a subject or an object is self-evident.

These symbolizations illustrate the way in which the changing of a sentence from the active to the passive turn means the shifting about from the lower to the upper storey in the diagram in **33**.3 as if we turned it round V as a pivot. This reversal is made possible by the fact that an object is really what has been called "a subject thrown into the background" (PhilGr 160).

37. 2. Infinitive.

Some languages have developed a passive infinitive, I^b. But the active infinitive is sometimes used in such a way that the meaning seems to be rather passive than active, in our symbols thus $I^{a/b}$. Above, **17**.4, however, an attempt has been made to avoid that notation in cases like *a house to let.* Similarly in F. "J'ai entendu chanter cette chanson", in which some grammarians (e.g. Sechehaye, Struct. log.) see a passive import in contrast to "J'ai entendu chanter cette actrice", where it is purely active. In "Je l'ai vu battre" the infinitive thus "suivant la circonstance" is active or passive.

In G. "Ich habe das lied singen hören" *singen,* too, is called "passi-visch" (See, e.g., Andresen, Sprachrichtigkeit 122). See my transcriptions in **17**.4.

37. 3. Participle, etc.

Active and passive participles are found in many languages, here denoted Y^a and Y^b respectively.[1] But in **21**.2 a few examples were given, in which the form and meaning were not congruent, so that we have to write $Y^{b/a}$.

In an analogous way the (active) gerund and nexus-substantive may in some cases have a passive import, so that we have to write $G^{a/b}$ and $X^{a/b}$, see **19**.2 and **20**.1.

CHAPTER 38.

Regimen. Recipient.

38. 1. Regimen.

It is customary in English grammars to speak of the object, not only of a verb, but also of a preposition (in the house), and I have in previous books used the same terminology. Correspondingly Seche-haye (Structure Log. 80) uses the word *transitif,* not only of verbs, but of prepositions, adjectives, etc. Cf. also what is said in PhilGr 88 f. on particles used as adverbs (intransitively), as prepositions (transitively, governing a word) and conjunctions (transitively, governing a clause). In spite of this obvious analogy I now think it best to restrict the term object to what is governed by a verb (including "verbids": infinitive, gerund, nexus-substantive, participle, and on the other hand, also including verbal complexes, W) and thus to use the symbols O and *O* exclusively for items governed by such words or their analogues. Thus I deviate from my earlier practice in which the term *object* was used for anything that is governed by a preposition: *the house* in combinations like *in, at,*

---

[1] In *I have seen the castle,* F. *J'ai vu le château* the participle has lost its passive import; in this work *have seen* and *ai vu* are taken as (active) units (V). G. *Ich habe das schloss gesehen* must accordingly be written S v O V.

over, by, under, to the house, etc. This I now call the *regimen* of the
preposition. It would be very awkward to use the symbol O for such
a regimen. Among other inconveniences it would create a great
many conflicts, e.g. in combinations like "the massacre of Christians
by Chinese", which we now conveniently symbolize X pO pS. A
special symbol for regimen in this sense is quite superfluous, as the
reader will have seen in numerous examples in Part I, in which p1
is written when the preposition governs an ordinary primary;
further, according to circumstances, pP, pI, pG, pX, etc. When
the preposition governs not a single, but a composite regimen neces-
sitating the use of the symbol ( ), 1 must be inserted between p and
the parenthesis, e.g. after seeing you p1(GO), sans vous voir p1(OI),
after he had gone p1(SV), etc.

It is not customary but, I think, legitimate to call *as* a preposition
in such combinations as "he lived as a saint", see examples in **9**.5 and
12.5.

38. 2. Recipient.

In conventional grammar the term *object* is further used for
what is governed by an adjective. Here, too, I have avoided the
term object in the present work and have adopted instead the term
Recipient, abbreviated R. The examples given in Ch. **11** are, I think,
sufficiently clear without any long explanation. R is seen to be
chiefly used where Latin, German, etc. have a dative which is not
governed by a transitive verb. In
G. Es ist mir unangenehm (nützlich, möglich), etc., one might say
that *mir* is the indirect object of the verbal complex *ist* + the adjective, but my chief reason for not using the symbol O here is that
in some cases such a dative is joined to an adjunct adjective: *ein
mir unangenehmer auftrag*, etc., where *O* would not seem appropriate; also in the other combinations there collected it seems best
to have a separate symbol, independent of those used with verbs.

It will be noticed that R even more than an object is similar to
a tertiary.

When the adjective is a kind of participle it may have O, see
21.4.

CHAPTER 39.
Verbids.
39. 1. Infinitive.

An infinitive according to circumstances is a primary, a secondary, or a tertiary, but it so far participates in the characteristics of the finite verb that it can take objects and tertiaries even when the infinitive itself is a primary, see above **34**.5. The infinitive is a primary, when it is a subject or an object. As a predicative it may be either a primary, in cases like "To see her is to adore her", or a secondary, as in "You are to go there", or F. "Ceci est à refaire", just as when it is an adjunct: "You are the man to go there", "A house to let", F. "Une chose à considérer", etc. Examples above **17**.3.

In these applications, when the infinitive is a secondary, whether as a predicative or as an adjunct, the infinitive is virtually a kind of participle and might therefore be symbolized as Y. Here it implies, but does not really denote a nexus.

When an infinitive stands as a tertiary it is generally in many languages preceded by a preposition. Examples above Ch. **18**. (But the preposition which originally served to indicate this role of the infinitive, as purpose, etc., tends to become a fixed part of the infinitive, even when the infinitive stands as subject or object).

39. 2. Y.

The letter Y is used in this system as a common denomination for what implies a nexus, though not really denoting one. It thus comprises both participles and agent-nouns (nomina agentis). Participles most often have secondary rank (*a barking dog, a cut flower*), but may also be used as primaries, as in "Separate firmly the known from the unknown | the women took care of the wounded | He is still in the land of the living".

Agent-nouns are substantives; like other substantives they most often stand as primaries, though nothing hinders them from occasionally being secondaries or tertiaries.

When nothing is said expressly of the rank of Y, it is a primary; if it is secondary the symbol 2(Y) is used except when Y is accompanied by a 3, which implies that Y is itself 2: a well-dressed child $3Y^b1$, a loud-crying child $3Y1$.

Both active participles and agent-nouns retain the capacity of the verbs from which they are derived, of taking objects, but while participles can take them immediately (in the accusative and dative in those languages that distinguish these cases), agent-nouns generally take them in the genitive. Examples of such Y O²'s are given in **21**. It is well-known that Latin made a distinction between *amans patriam* (participle) and *amans patriae* (agent-noun), the latter denoting a more permanent activity or feeling.

Tertiaries may become secondaries with Y in the same way as with X: A *constant* reader of the Times 2(3)Y pO, they are *dreadful* critics of everything English, etc.

As it is our general principle to regard notion rather than form in our symbols and to disregard the difference between word-classes, the symbol Y sometimes stands for a substantive, sometimes for an adjective, and sometimes for a participle, provided they mean the same thing 'he who does, or that which does' what is implied in the corresponding verb. Now as the principle just referred to has actually been broken by the adoption of the symbol I for the infinitive, it cannot be wondered at that there is at times a certain overlapping between I and Y. When an infinitive is used as a secondary, either as adjunct or as predicative, it may (as already remarked) be considered a kind of Y. The first examples given in **18**.6 of infinitives in compounds might have been written with Y instead of I, and inversely those Y-compounds in which the base of the verb is used (**21**.5), might have been written with I, at any rate as far as English is concerned. If we have written them with Y, it is on account of the meaning; compare F. *brise-glace* with E. *ice-breaker*. The historical explanation of such compounds, whether originally containing an imperative or not, has been disputed, see among other treatments that by Darmesteter, reprinted in Spitzer's collection Meisterwerke der romanischen sprachwissenschaft I. 232 ff. (1929).[1] Dan. *drikkepenge, spillebord, sovekammer* ought to be written 2(I)-1; but this is not true of the corresponding G. *trinkgeld, spieltisch, schlafzimmer,* which we can symbolize only as 2-1 without deciding whether the first element is to be considered nominal or verbal.

39. 3. Gerund.

The English gerund in *-ing* is originally a nexus-substantive (X) and still shares some of the peculiarities of X, see next paragraph;

---

[1] *Breakfast* is isolated from *break* and *fast* in pronunciation, inflexion and meaning and cannot therefore any longer be symbolized Y-O, but only 1.

but the historic development (for which, till the full treatment in MEG vol. V appears, I must refer to the short sketch in Soc. f. Pure English, Tract 25, 1926) has gone in the same direction as the pre-historic development of the infinitive, so that now it can have an object and a subject without putting them in the genitive. Illustrations in Ch. **19**. The gerund itself may be subject or object and then is a primary, as also when it is P in cases like "Seeing is believing" and when it is governed by a preposition. It seems to be a secondary in those cases only when it enters into compounds, **19.4**.

39. 4. Nexus-Substantive.

We next come to what I have called nexus-substantives and here denote by the letter X (taken from ne*x*us). These, in all the languages that possess them, are treated exactly as ordinary substantives, in flexion and syntax, and yet they fall outside the ordinary definition of "substantives". I shall not here repeat what I have said at some length in PhilGr 136—143 and 169—172, cf. also 200, 211, 284, but only deal with a few salient traits.[1]

The chief peculiarity of the nexus-substantives may be expressed in Nietzschean phrase: "umvertung aller werte", for even such "airy nothings" as *liberty* or *love* or *suggestion* are treated as if they were things, with the grammatical consequences that

(a) a nexus is represented as a junction,
(b) primaries (subjects and objects) are made into secondaries by being put in the genitive, or else made into prepositional adjuncts,[2]
(c) tertiaries are equally made into secondaries (adverbs into adjectives).

Thus "the doctor (1) arrived (2) speedily (3)" becomes "the doctor's (2) speedy (2) arrival (1)".

For examples it may suffice to refer to Ch. **20**.

It is well-known that the indiscriminate use of the genitive for the

---

[1] Sechehaye, Struct. log. 102, 103, is not far from my own views, note especially his term "transposition", which recalls my own words (PhilGr 92) that they are "specially devised for the purpose of transposing words from one word-class to another".

[2] In speaking of subject (S) in connexion with X I am in agreement with Brunot, who in "La pensée et la langue", p. 227 ff. extends the term *sujet* to cases like *"ton* départ" and "le succès *ministériel"*.

subject as well as for the object may in some cases lead to ambiguity (amor matris) ; on the way in which languages remedy this danger, see PhilGr 171.

The following extreme examples of shiftings by means of nexus-substantives were given in PhilGr 91; they are reprinted here with the appropriate symbols; by the numeral 2 is everywhere meant 2(3) :

He moved astonishingly fast S V 4 3.

He moved with astonishing rapidity S V p1(2X).

His movements were astonishingly rapid $S(S_2{}^2X)$ V P(32).

His rapid movements astonished us $S(S_2{}^22X)$ V O.

His movements astonished us by their rapidity .

$$S(S_2{}^2X) \text{ V O p1}(S^2X).$$

The rapidity of his movements was astonishing

$$S(Xp1(S_2{}^2X)) \text{ V P(Y)}.$$

The rapidity with which he moved astonished us

$$S(X \ 2(p1^c \ S_2 \ V)) \text{ V O}.$$

He astonished us by moving rapidly S V O p1(G3).

He astonished us by his rapid movements S V O p1$(S_2{}^22X)$.

He astonished us by the rapidity of his movements

$$\text{S V O p1}(XpS_2{}^2X_2).$$

In German it is not only the object which with a finite verb would be in the accusative, but also the datival object that is made into a genitive adjunct to a nexus-substantive : zur beiwohnung des zweikampfs, die nachfolge der lehre Christi, die nachforschung der wahrheit, etc. Many examples in Paul's Gramm. 3.288, who objects to it ("ungehöriger weise"). He likewise gives examples in which the genitive used with the verb is retained with the nexus-substantive : die erinnerung des vergangenen, beraubung der menschlichen gesell-schaft,—and examples in which the finite verb would be combined with a prepositional phrase : ein andenken meiner teuren ahnen, die stärkste abneigung der liebe.

Only exceptionally does a nexus-substantive admit the same case as the verb from which it is formed, thus the accusative in the often-mentioned Plautine questions "Quid tibi hanc tractio'st?" / "Quid tibi hanc curatiost rem?"; the dative in L. Obtemperatio legibus, and Gk. he tou theou dosis humin 'god's gift to you'. In Bulgarian the nexus-substantives in *-anie* may take the accusative; in Danish we have "tagen del i lykken", etc. On this and the Latin gerund see PhilGr 140—141.

CHAPTER 40.

Clauses.

40. 1. That.

In MEG III Ch. 8 I argued at some length against recognizing *that* as a relative *pronoun* on the same footing as *who* and *which*: it is to be regarded as the same word that we have in "I know that you mentioned the man", namely as a connecting particle (conjunction) which in many cases can be dispensed with. In consequence of this view this *that* should be symbolized differently from *who* and *which*. In "the man that we saw" we should not write 12(O^c S V) as we do for "the man whom we saw": *that* cannot here be called an object, and neither is it a subject in "the man that saw us". The easiest way is therefore to write nothing but 3^c for *that*. As this view, however, is not shared by all grammarians, I have in Ch. **23**.4 availed myself of the possibility my system affords of indicating two alternative grammatical conceptions of the same phenomena by means of the oblique stroke / , writing 3$^{c\cdot}$ before and O^c (or S^c, etc.) after the stroke. The same remark applies to relative *as* and *but* (MEG III Ch. 9). Apart from this indication of two alternative analyses we must have complete conformity in the symbols for combinations like:

The man that we saw

Such men as we saw

The man we saw.

40. 2. Contact-Clauses.

There are two ways of symbolizing relative clauses without any connective in English and the Scandinavian languages, one in which a non-existent relative pronoun is denoted by means of ^{o}:

I have got the book you want S V O(12(O^{co} S$_2$ V))—

and another, which is more in conformity with the natural feeling; for, as a matter of fact, *the book* is felt as belonging to what follows as well as to what precedes (apo koinou): S V O(O$_2$* 2(S$_2$ V*)).

Here the stars connect together *the book* and *want* and thus show that *the book* is the object of *want*. But it should be noted expressly that the object of the first verb (*have got*) is not *the book* in itself, as so many grammarians say or imply in their analysis, but really the whole combination *the book you want. The book* is thus at the same time a full object (of *want*) and part of an object (of *have got*). This is in exact agreement with the analysis of other combinations advocated by me here and elsewhere (we found *them guilty,* made *her laugh,* etc.). Correspondingly *the book you want* is S in "the book you want is here", etc.

I must confess that a sentence like "This is all there is" is not easy to symbolize; the weak *there* generally presupposes a subject—but "there is all" is impossible. Perhaps S V P(S₂3V) might do with the sign for the full *there.*

Examples of contact-clauses after *it is* see **25**.6.

40. 3. Various Remarks.

The symbol ᶜ, the reader may have remarked, does not stand for any particular word-class: Sᶜ and Oᶜ are relative pronouns, 3ᶜ according to circumstances is a relative adverb or a conjunction, 1ᶜ is a relative pronoun which is neither subject nor object, but still a primary.

When *after* or *before* introduces a clause, we may write them either 3ᶜ like ordinary conjunctions or else as prepositions p, but in that case it is necessary to insert 1 as the regimen of the preposition, which then is interpreted by means of the following parenthesis: he came before I left, Dan. han kom før jeg rejste

$$S \; V \; 3(3^c S_2 V) \; \text{or} \; S \; V \; p1(S_2 V).$$

Note here and in other instances of conjunctional clauses the obligatory insertion of 3 before the clause as a sign of its being a tertiary in the sentence as a whole.

Note also the distinction between the two *when*'s, corresponding to G. *wenn* and *wann,* the former denoted 3ᶜ and the latter 3ᶜ? See an example of both together **22**.3 and compare the two applications of *which. How* may be both 3ᶜ, 3ᶜ? and 3ᶜ!

CHAPTER 41.

Conclusion.

41. 1. Latent.

The symbol ⁰ stands for something that is "latent", i.e. not expressed in the sentence analyzed. With regard to my use of this symbol let me first say that I am opposed to what might be termed the "ellipsomania" of some grammarians who speak of ellipsis in season and out of season as a sort of panacea to explain a great many things which either need no explanation or else are not explained, or not sufficiently explained, by the assumption that something is "understood". Some writers will speak of ellipsis only when some element which was found in an earlier period has now dropped out ("diachronic ellipsis")[1], but most grammarians use the term also of "synchronic ellipsis" and very often imply that an expression is really incomplete (logically or grammatically) without the element which they supply and which thus is considered "missing" and said to be "understood". This latter English term, by the way, is not very felicitous (witness the possibility of saying, "the writer's words would be more easily understood if there was not so much understood"); it should be rather "under-understood" corresponding to the expressions used in other languages: F. *sous-entendre,* It. *sottintendere,* Sp. *sobrentender,* Dan. *underforstå.*

Pretty often the supposition of an ellipsis is totally uncalled for, and then, of course, the symbol ^{0} has not been used in our analyses. Thus nothing is gained by saying that in "I believe he is ill" (**22**.1) the conjunction *that* is understood: historically we must say that a conjunction has never been needed in such collocations, and logically the expression is complete in itself: the object of "I believe" is "he is ill", which if standing alone would be a sentence in its own right, but is now dependent and is therefore termed a clause (G. nebensatz). Neither are those grammarians right who would have it that in "Who steals my purse steals trash" an "antecedent" (he) is understood before the relative pronoun. The whole relative clause is here the subject of "steals trash". Similarly in the sentences immediately following this example in **22**.5. As a matter of fact it would be quite impossible to supply an antecedent before *whoever* or *what* (*whatever*).

But the misuse of the term ellipsis should not detain us from a legitimate use, and I hope readers will approve my moderate use of the symbol ^{0}.

When I write S^0 or O^0, etc., I do not mean to say that something is missing or should properly be there. To take examples from **8**.2 and **8**.4; no Englishman in saying "he is dressing" or "they meet" has a feeling that anything is left out, or that the expression is incomplete, and if I write $S \ V \ O^0(S)$ in one case and $S \ V \ O^0(S_x)$

---

[1] What is called "suffixe zéro" seems in most cases to fall under this head, see **29**.1.

in the other case, what I mean is simply that *if* there had been an object (as usually after such "transitive" verbs) it would have been in one case "himself" (O=S) and in the other "one another" (S_x). In the exclamations of deprecation (**26**.7) I write ^{no} to indicate that the meaning (implied by the tone) is negative, but that no negative word is actually used in the sentence. (By a curious coincidence these two letters n and o together seem to furnish the answer *no* to the question preceding them, but that is quite accidental). On the relative contact-clauses, in which scholars are apt to think that a relative pronoun is "understood", see above **40**.2.

If *straw* is used of a kind of hat = 'straw-hat' this is symbolized $1(2-1^0)$ to indicate that if *hat* had been expressed it would have been the last (primary) element of a compound of which *straw* is the first (secondary) part. (Above **6**.8). In compounds like *Austria-Hungary* the sign $\&^0$ placed between the two equipollent components shows that if there had been anything between them, it would have been "and".

Very often the expression would become quite unidiomatic if the item marked with ^{0} were to be expressed. Anyhow, it would generally weaken the force of an utterance if the speaker were to say explicitly everything that the hearer will easily understand. This is especially the case in answers. If A asks: "Will he take photos when he comes this afternoon?" the answer "he will" means "he will take photos when he comes this afternoon". Above (**18**.5), I have noted only S V $O^0(I)$, but not that this latent infinitive may have an object and other complements. "Nothing" as answer to the question "What did he say?" is sufficiently symbolized O instead of $S^0 V^0 O$, etc. Cf. also **26**.3 and **34**.3 and 5.

What is said here, will probably suffice to explain both the use and the omission of the ^{0} symbol (Note **9**.6 Predicative without a verb). But there are, of course, doubtful cases in which one may hesitate whether to employ it or no.

41. 2. Possible Extension of the System.

In constructing my system I have, of course, been constantly asking myself if it would not be possible to extend it to other fields of syntactic investigation. I ought perhaps to have had a section about verbal compounds of the type *overlook: he overlooked the field* = 'he looked over the field' S p*-V O*, similarly Dan. *han overgår sin bror*, G. *er übertrifft seinen bruder*. But this would only complicate matters, and generally the notation S V O is felt to be perfectly satisfactory. In "he overlooked the error" = 'failed to see' the symbol S V O seems, as a matter of fact, to be the only possible analysis, and the same is true of most verbal compounds.

I have also considered, but rejected, the use of such symbols as = for *as* and > for *than* in sentences like "He is as big as John" and "he is bigger than John", where I now use only 3ᶜ (see **24**.7), which says nothing but only connects the item with what precedes.

As soon as we try to step outside the syntactic fields circumscribed in **28**.5 we meet with unsurmountable difficulties, all of them due to the innumerable differences of linguistic structure which militate against any generally applicable symbols. Let me illustrate this with one example. One of the simplest syntactic distinctions seems to be that between singular and plural. One might imagine the rule that the singular should always be unmarked and the plural marked by the sign + placed under the symbol, thus

He gave her a ring S V *O* O

They gave her a ring S V *O* O
$$_{+}$$

He gave them a ring Ṡ V *O* O
$$_{+}$$

They gave them rings S V *O* O, etc.
$$_{+}\ _{+}\ _{+}$$

But on closer inspection various difficulties arise. First, what is one to do with V? Should we mark the difference between (he) *is* and (they) *are*? The distinction is observed in many languages, in English generally in the present tense, but not in the preterit, and in the present tense only in the third person. In Danish it has disappeared, and indeed it is superfluous (and really logically erroneous), as demonstrated by the fact that all recent systems of constructed languages (esperanto, ido, occidental, novial) make no distinction, and feel no want of any, in their verbs according to the number of the subject. The real logical application of the plural idea to a verb is found in frequentatives such as L. *cantito* 'sing frequently', Ru. *strĕlivat'* 'fire several shots, shoot continually' (MEG II. 6.9). Further difficulties are found with collectives (the family...it...its, or they...their), with mass-words (butter, oats, brain(s), verse, measles), and with generic expressions (a (the) tiger is cruel, tigers are cruel, etc.).

Similar, only greater, difficulties would be found were we to devise general syntactic symbols for such categories as time (tense), person, or gender. On case see above, Ch. **30**. All things considered, I feel that I have done well in restricting my symbolization to the categories dealt with in this work.

41. 3. Notes on "The Philosophy of Grammar".

In this book I have so often taken up again the same matters that I dealt with in my previous work "The Philosophy of Grammar" (Allen & Unwin, 1924, abbreviated PhilGr), criticizing, modifying, or amplifying my former views and expressions, that it will be found useful here to collect all such passages and refer to the corresponding chapters and sections in the present book.

(P. refers to pages in PhilGr.)

P. 49 French superlative **29**.2(5).

P. 56 Form—Function—Notion **29**.1.

P. 75 Substantives on the whole more special than adjectives;
P. 76 note extension of substantives and adjectives;
P. 79 numerical test; greater complexity of qualities denoted by substantives **31**.3 note.

P. 85 Quantifiers **32**.

P. 85 Relative *that* **40**.1.

P. 89 Conjunction and preposition **24**.4 and **40**.3.

P. 91 Adjectives and adverbs with nexus-substantives **39**. 4.

P. 96 ff. Rank **31**.

P. 96 For "one word of supreme importance" read "one unit of supreme grammatical importance" and see definition **31**.3.

P. 96 the example "a certainly not very cleverly worded remark" criticized **31**.2.

P. 96 Only three ranks distinguished **31**.2.

P. 98 Substantives as adjuncts; better coordinatior **31**.4 and **31**.8.

P. 100 Infinitives as primaries **33**.5 and **34**.5.

P. 103 Clause better defined "a member of a sentence having a form similar to that of a sentence" **40**; see also **23**—**25**.

P. 104 "What you say is true" **22**.5; **41**.1; cf. MEG III 3.1.

P. 107 line 12 from bottom read "the oblique cases (or rather some of them) are devices for turning the substantive...into a secondary...or tertiary", etc.

P. 111 "That noble heart of hers" **4**.4; see also S.P.E. Tract 25 and MEG III. 1.5.

P. 113 Quantifier **32** and **5**.

P. 114 French partitive article **7**.5.

P. 114—116 Difference between junction and nexus **33**; rank in nexus **33**.4. N.B.

P. 117—120 Infinitival nexus **15**.

P. 120 f. Nominal sentences **9**.6.

P. 122 Nexus-object **14**.1.

P. 124 "Post urbem conditam"**14** .4.

P. 126 "Too many cooks" **14**.2.

P. 126 Nexus subjunct (tertiary) **14**.5 and **34**.2.

P. 129 Nexus of deprecation **26**.7.

P. 131 Predicative **35**.

P. 133 ff. Nexus-substantive **39**.4 and **20**.

P. 137 Cognate object **12**.8.

P. 139 Infinitive and gerund **39**.1 and 3.

P. 141 One member-nexus **34**.3.

P. 145 ff. Subject **34**.

P. 150 Subject comparatively definite **34**.6.

P. 153 Quotation from Keats **35**.3.

P. 154 Existential sentences ("there is") **34**.6—9.

P. 156 Object, definition **36**.

P. 158 Object makes verb more definite **33**.6.

P. 159 O/P **9**.7.

P. 160 f. O/S **8**.8.

P. 161 Reciprocal **8**.4.

P. 161 Two objects **36**.5 ff.

P. 162 Object with adjective and adverb **38**.1 (**R**).

P. 164 Passive **37**.

P. 169 "Pickpocket" **21**.5.

P. 169 Subject and object with nexus-substantive **20** and **39** .4.

P. 170 Passive infinitive **37**.2, **15**.2, **16**.

P. 172 ff. Case **30**.

P. 181 French partitive article **7**.5.

P. 183 "Dem kerl sein hut" **12**.4.

P. 211 Plural of verbal idea **41**.3.

P. 221 Reflexive and reciprocal **8**.2—4.

P. 245 French superlative **29**.2(5).

P. 282 line 4 (*will*) read: "still in some combinations retains some trace of the original meaning".

P. 301 Classification of utterances **13**.

P. 306 One-member sentence **34**.3 and **35**.1.

P. 309 Suppression **41**.1 and **26**.

P. 311 Signboards, etc. **26**.

Addendum to **8**.8.

Further examples of It. *si* = F. *on*: se si è cristiani si ha il dovere d'obbediare a suo padre (Fogazzaro)/Perchè non ti si vede in nessun luogo? (Verga). Sp. *se*: suelen verse esas condescencias con los grandes, mientras se persigue sin piedad á los pequeños (Galdós). In America educated people say "se vende frutos", etc., see Lenz, La Oración y sus Partes, 2. ed. 89,252.

Index

The numbers given refer to section numbers of the text.